THE
Hawaiian Quilt

The Tradition Continues

OTHER BOOKS BY THE AUTHORS

*Poakalani Hawaiian Quilt
Cushion Patterns & Designs
Volume One*

*Poakalani Hawaiian Quilt
Cushion Patterns & Designs
Volume Two*

*Poakalani Hawaiian Quilt
Cushion Patterns & Designs
Volume Three*

*Poakalani Hawaiian Quilt
Cushion Patterns & Designs
Volume Four*

*The Hawaiian Quilt—
A Spiritual Experience*

THE
Hawaiian Quilt

The Tradition Continues

by Hawai'i's Quilting Family

POAKALANI SERRAO

JOHN SERRAO

RAELENE CORREIA

CISSY SERRAO

MUTUAL PUBLISHING

Library of Congress Cataloging-in-Publication Data

The Hawaiian quilt : the tradition continues / by Hawai'i's Quilting Family Poakalani
Serrao ... [et al.].
p. cm.
ISBN 1-56647-835-9 (softcover : alk. paper)
1. Quilting--Hawaii. 2. Quilts--Hawaii. I. Serrao, Poakalani.
TT835.S4536 2007
746.46'04109969--dc22
2007019121

Second Printing, April 2009
Third Printing, March 2012

ISBN-10: 1-56647-835-9
ISBN-13: 978-1-56647-835-9

Design by Julie Chun Design

Mutual Publishing, LLC
1215 Center Street, Suite 210
Honolulu, Hawai'i 96816
Ph: (808) 732-1709 / Fax: (808) 734-4094
email: info@mutualpublishing.com
www.mutualpublishing.com

Printed in Taiwan

This book is a blending of many hearts.

The Quilting teachers in Poakalani, John, Tuffy & Cissy.
The Designer in John and, most of all, the quilters.

TO ALL OUR QUILTERS,
We have always believed that a quilt pattern is just lines on a piece of paper until someone gives it life. Thank you for breathing life back into a once dying art by continuing to perpetuate our quilting traditions.

HEARTFELT GRATITUDE TO:
Gillian Barnett, Noriko Bartek, Sanae Furusawa, Eriko Furukawa, Tokiko Furukawa, June Gerber, Junko Haba, Phyllis Hirata, Tamako Ho, Ale Hogue, Colleen Holmes; Holoholo Club of Japan members: Mitsue Baba, Mariko Takahashi, Kiyomi Itou, Miyoko Itou, Chikako Asano, Wakako Shionoya; Takako Jenkins, Takako Jinushi, Kaori Kaneshiro, Tomoko Kato, Keiko Kawai, Lily Kobayashi, Kimi Kumagai, Wilma Makilan, Cecile Medeiros, Mie Morimoto, Nobuko Nakagawa, Keiko Nakamura, Yoko Nakayama, Yoko Niizawa, Yuko Nishiwaki Chiyo Narashima, Anne-Marie Norton, Tomiko Okada, Arisa Okano, Yuki Orikasa, Keiko Sakamoto, Doris Shibuya, Susie Sugi, Yoshimi Suzuki, Toshie Takashima, Mitsue Toi, Hiroko Vaughan, Tia Waxman, and Lynette Yee for allowing us to share your quilts with the world.

A SPECIAL THANK YOU TO:
The Friends of 'Iolani Palace, The Royal Hawaiian Shopping Center, Kamehameha Schools, Mission Houses Museum, Queen Emma Summer Palace, Outrigger Hotels & Resorts, and Mutual Publishing for giving us the opportunity and venue to teach our art.

MOST OF ALL TO:
Joseph Serrao, John Serrao Jr., Aalene Correia, Thea Correia, and Aaron Correia, who complete our family.

And…in memory of Tutu Hattie Serrao and Tutu Caroline Correa for sharing their quilting traditions.

Our first quilting book, *The Hawaiian Quilt—A Spiritual Experience* was written to share with everyone not only the technical steps of creating a Hawaiian quilt but also the spiritual meaning behind the different sections of a quilt. This book is a continuation of that first journey. We are proud to share with you our quilters, their stories, and artistic work through their quilted masterpieces. Enjoy the experience and then learn to create your own masterpiece.

Table of Contents

PREFACE

The Hawaiian Quilt and Where It All Began   x

THE HAWAIIAN QUILT...THE TRADITION CONTINUES

Pele, The Fire Goddess   1
'Ulu   2
Haku Lei   3
Lei Aloha   4
Kapa Kuiki O Ke Kai   5
Ocean & Shell Series   6
Hibiscus   7
Kapiko O Lē'ahi   8
He Inoa No Na Ali'i   9
Mahiole   10
Nā Koa 'Uhane O Hawai'i   10
King Kamehameha I   11
Nā Mea O Nā Ali'i   12
Ka Māmalahoe Kanāwai   12
Queen Ka'ahumanu   13
Nānā I Ke Ku'uipo   14
Na Mele O Hawai'i   14
Kamehameha III   15
Pōpoki 'Okika   16
King Kalākaua   17
Queen Lili'uokalani   18
Kanikapila   19
Monsterra   20
Hawaiian Island Sampler   21
Pua Melia   22
Nā Pua Onaona   23
Lei Pua Melia   24
Nā Pali O Ko'olau   25
Bird of Paradise   26

Pikapua O Puʻuwai	27
Honu ʻAukai	28
Iʻa O Ke Kai	28
Lilikoʻi	29
Tokiko's Mele	30
Ti Leaf	30
Na Aliʻi O ʻAwapuhi	31
Mele Kalikimaka	32
Kukui ʻOhana O Cecile	32
ʻUlu	33
Na Koa	33
Hilo Hanakahi	34
Hilo Beauty	35
The Garden of Aloha	36
Kukui Ula Hale O Queen Emma	36
Kumulaʻau Niu	37
Tropical Hawaiʻi	38
Turtles & Dolphins	38
Tropical Paradise	39
Pua Nui O Ka Punahou	40
ʻEhu Kai	41
Bombax	42
Plumeria	43
Anthurium	44
ʻŪlei Berries	45
African Tulip	46
Pua Kuʻipo	47
Silversword	48
Kaomi Mālie	49
Anthurium	50
Taro	50
Hearts & Roses	51
Star Plumeria	51
Sakura	52
He Pule Kākou	53
Loke Lani	53
Bird of Paradise	54
Kuʻu Home Me Kela ʻAo ʻAo	55
Monsterra	56

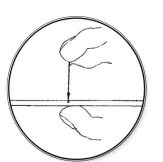

Hibiscus 57
Shower Tree 58
Orchids 59
Kapa Pohopoho 60
Monsterra & Gecko 61
Climbing Turtles 61
Mele Nai'a 62
Takako's Goldfish 63
Hibiscus & Griffin 63
Mele Nai'a 64
Hula Hula Nai'a 65
He'e 65
'Ohana Nai'a 66
King Pineapple 67
Ku'u Hae Owyhee 68

BEGINNING YOUR MASTERPIECE

Supply List 69

SEWING YOUR MASTERPIECE

Preparing and Joining your Fabric 72
Laying Out Your Pattern & Cutting Your Design 73
Appliquéing 74
Quilting 75
Reverse Appliqué 77
Patterns 79

PHOTO ALBUM

94

GLOSSARY

96

About the Authors

99

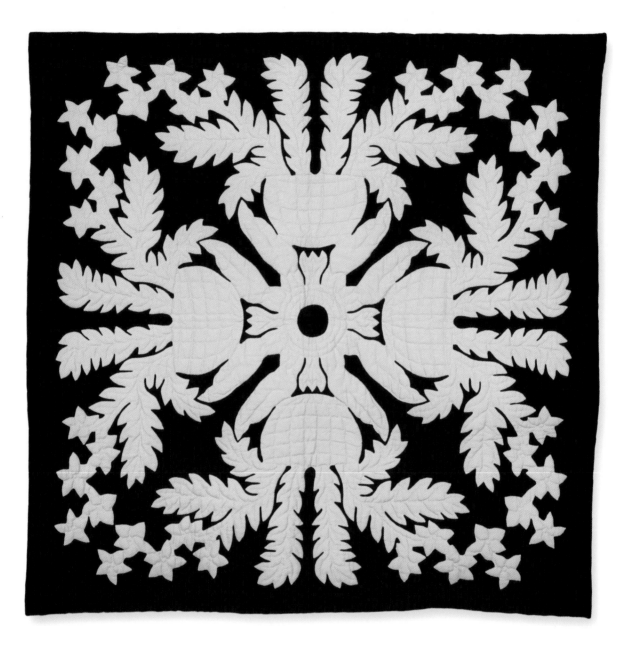

The Hands of Creation

APPLIQUÉD AND QUILTED BY Doris Shibuya, Honolulu, Hawai`i
PERSONAL DESIGN BY John Serrao
45" x 45"

Ho'onani i ka Makua Mau	Praise to the eternal father
Ke Keiki me ka 'Uhane nō	The son with the spirit indeed
Ke Akua Mau	God Eternal,
Ho'omaika'i pū	Bless together
Kō kēia ao, kō kēlā ao	Today, tomorrow, everyday

Preface: The Hawaiian Quilt...
and Where It All Began

LEGENDS SPEAK OF HOW THE HAWAIIAN PEOPLE CAME from the heavens to occupy a land of great beauty that was bountiful with all of life's necessities, and it was here that they lived many generations in harmony with god, nature, and each other. While living in this serene land it was also a custom for the people of Hawai'i to document extraordinary events, spiritual teachings, cultural traditions, and genealogies. But the people of old Hawai'i did not have a written language that we know of today. Instead, they used a language that was taught to them by their heavenly ancestors, a language that documented a people rich in culture and spirituality.

The language that the Hawaiians used was symbolic in design and also melodic in verse and song. The history of those ancient people, their legends, and genealogy were recorded in chants they recited, in the rhythmic motions of their bodies as they danced the hula, in the petroglyphs they carved throughout the Islands, and on their calabashes, war clubs, and utensils. Even the feather capes that they wore proudly also held their family crests, as well as the tattoos they pressed onto their bodies. The symbols and designs of old Hawai'i were also stamped onto tapa that was worn daily and used as warm coverings during the cool evenings.

After many generations had passed, spiritual seers of those great ancient people prophesied that the Hawaiians' harmonious balance would be broken, and foresaw their ultimate demise and extinction. This prediction came to pass when the first foreigners from far-off lands came to Hawai'i's shores.

In the 1770s foreigners of a different culture and lifestyle arrived in the Islands. They fell in love with its beauty and decided to stay and also call it their home. They then proceeded to force upon the Hawaiians to adapt to their foreign lifestyle—a lifestyle that would end that harmonious balance between the physical and spiritual world, a new lifestyle that stopped the worship of their gods and introduced a new Christian God, a new lifestyle that would wash away the old symbols of their life and ancestors.

Soon new forms of storage containers were introduced on the Islands and the Hawaiians stopped creating their wooden bowls where their special family designs were engraved. Petroglyphs were no longer needed; the feather capes were no longer made and Western fabric replaced the tapa. The designs and symbols of old that were pounded into the tapa were lost to a new way of life. Eventually a new written language was introduced but it did not contain that unique inner meaning of their ancient tongue. The Hawaiians lost their past in a new world that was unfamiliar to them.

Around the 1820s a new form of sewing was introduced to the Hawaiian women—quilting. Missionaries taught the Hawaiians the skill of patchwork quilting with new softer fabric, modern needles, and thread. The native women learned this new domestic duty but they missed their ancient designs that spoke of their family history and the days of old. While the women sewed their blankets they realized that this new craft could be remodified to reflect their old language. So the native women tailored the sewing to reflect the symbols of their past. In the early 1860s quilts began to appear with designs of that old Hawai'i before the arrival of the foreigners. Quilts with symmetrical medallion centers began to emerge throughout the Island chain. The women of that Hawai'i once again were placing back into their work symbols of those long lost days. Once again the preservation of the culture, historical legends, their inner desires, and their future desires were being quilted into what we know today as **the Hawaiian quilt**.

The Hawaiian Quilt
the Tradition Continues...

Every Hawaiian quilt tells a story. The story is interwoven in the design, revealed through the colors of the fabric, captured in the intricate quilting lines and spirit filled in the labor of the quilter. So in that spirit we share with you the story of Hawai'i, the culture of our people, the desires and masterpieces of our quilting class.

Pele, The Fire Goddess

APPLIQUÉD AND QUILTED BY Gillian Barnett, Victoria, Canada
PERSONAL DESIGN BY John Serrao

90" x 90" Reverse Appliqué

HAWAIIAN QUILTS ARE ONE OF HAWAI'I'S MOST TREASURED ART FORMS FOR IT TELLS THE STORY of Hawai'i's gods, legends, traditions, and that simple way of life that has been long forgotten. One of those legends speaks of how Pele, the fire goddess, raised up the Islands from the ocean floor and made herself a home. This quilt was designed to show Pele in her awesome glory of fire looking into the center of the volcano. *The tradition of the Hawaiian quilt is to symmetrically fold your fabric and cut out the design in one piece. Reverse appliqué quilts are also cut in the old tradition and are fast becoming a unique contribution to Hawai'i's quilting tradition.*

ʻUlu

APPLIQUÉD AND QUILTED BY Yoko Niizawa, Honolulu, Hawaiʻi
COMMERCIAL CENTER DESIGN Caroline Correa Vintage Collection circa 1920
PERSONAL BORDER DESIGN BY John Serrao

108" x 108"

THE ABUNDANCE OF FLORAL AND FAUNA IN THE ISLANDS MADE WAY FOR A LARGE COLLECTION
of quilt patterns depicting Hawaiʻi's natural landscape, especially the ʻulu design. The Hawaiians
cultivated the ʻulu tree because the fruit was cooked and eaten as a starch with their meals, but the
quilters also loved the artistic leaves and large fruit that make it a perfect design for a quilt. *Many
people believed that if you made an ʻulu quilt first you would not want for any of life's necessities. Yoko
loved the story and the beauty of the ʻulu tree and wanted to make this pattern her first large quilt. Her
favorite part of making this design was quilting the leaves to make it look exactly like the real leaf.*

Haku Lei

APPLIQUÉD AND QUILTED BY Phyllis Hirata, Honolulu, Hawai`i
PERSONAL DESIGN BY John Serrao
90" x 90"

THE DELICATE LEAVES AND COLORFUL BLOSSOMS OF THE ISLANDS WERE CAREFULLY WEAVED AND braided to make the Hawaiian haku lei. Lei are given on every type of occasion including birthdays, anniversaries, weddings, graduations, and memorials. It is Hawai'i's custom to express friendship, gratitude, joy, and especially love. *Small leaves are never a popular motif for some quilters; the short points and deep valleys can be intimidating, but the final result is an artistic wonder.*

Lei Aloha

APPLIQUÉD AND QUILTED BY Doris Shibuya, Honolulu, Hawai`i
PERSONAL AND COMMERCIAL DESIGNS BY John Serrao
90" x 108" Sampler Quilt

EVERY QUILT TELLS A STORY, BUT A SAMPLER QUILT TELLS SEVERAL STORIES IN THE MANY BLOCKS
and designs that are incorporated into the quilt. The floral splendor of the Mokihana, Hinahina,
Loke Lani, Pua Melia, Monsterra, Hibiscus (Pua Aloalo), Pua Pākē, Pineapple, 'Ūlei
berries, Kukui Nut, Bird of Paradise, and 'Ulu are fashioned in a circular design.
*The traditional crosshatch quilting style is seen in the older Hawaiian
quilts and is widely used today on the panels of sampler quilts.*

Kapa Kuiki O Ke Kai
QUILTING BY THE SEA

APPLIQUÉD AND QUILTED BY Eriko Furukawa, Niigata, Japan
PERSONAL DESIGN BY John Serrao

90" x 90"

STORIES BEHIND PERSONAL QUILT DESIGNS SOMETIMES REVEAL A QUILTER'S TRUE PASSION. ERIKO is from Niigata, Japan, a city near the ocean. This quilt with its turtles and dolphins tells of her livelihood of teaching Hawaiian quilting near her home by the sea.

We always encourage our quilters to be consistent in their quilting stitches. It doesn't matter how big or small the stitches are —just make them uniformed throughout the quilt. Some of our quilters strive for exhibition quality quilts: this quilt has 12 top quilting stitches per inch.

Ocean & Shell Series

APPLIQUED AND QUILTED BY Yoko Nakayama, Honolulu, Hawai`i
PERSONAL DESIGNS BY John Serrao
45" x 45"

A HOME'S INTERIOR OFTEN INFLUENCES THE DESIGN AND COLORS OF A QUILT. YOKO'S HOME IS an aquarium of sea life and oceanic wonder from seashell lampshades to her new hand-quilted seascape panels of shells and dolphins. *Houses are getting smaller, and many quilters are now making the smaller 45" x 45" quilts as their masterpiece so it can be displayed proudly in their homes.*

Hibiscus

APPLIQUÉD AND QUILTED BY Toshie Takashima, Osaka, Japan
COMMERCIAL DESIGN BY John Serrao
90" x 90"

MANY PEOPLE BELIEVE THAT THE VIBRANT COLORS OF OUR ISLANDS, FROM THE LUSH GREEN
mountains and valleys to the bright flowers, influenced the colors of the Hawaiian quilts—bold,
bright, spiritual in design, and lively in color. *Everyone loves to peek at the backing fabric
of the quilts because it occasionally reveals the quilter's true spirit.*

Kapiko O Lēʻahi
THE CENTER OF DIAMOND HEAD

APPLIQUÉD AND QUILTED BY Sanae Fuchisawa, Honolulu, Hawaiʻi
Caroline Correa Vintage Quilt Collection circa 1920
90" x 90"

JUST OFF THE COAST OF DIAMOND HEAD, FISHERMEN OF OLD CAUGHT GREAT SCHOOLS OF ʻAHI
(tuna) to feed their families. This is the area they called Lēʻahi, the Hawaiian name for
Diamond Head. *The tradition of a solid color on a white background gives the quilt
a crisp clean look. The design becomes the focal point of the quilt and, in its simplicity,
is very soothing to the eyes. Unfortunately, many quilters know that working
with white can be difficult in keeping the quilt clean.*

He Inoa No Na Ali`i
IN HONOR OF THE VILLAGE CHIEF

APPLIQUÉD AND QUILTED BY Takako Jinushi, Tokyo, Japan
PERSONAL DESIGN BY John Serrao

60" x 90"

PRIOR TO KAMEHAMEHA I THERE WERE MANY VILLAGE CHIEFS WHO WORKED THE LAND BESIDE their people. The chief's royal status symbols of the kāhili and warrior helmet were designed into the quilt along with the taro plant and poi pounder, portraying the work of the common man. *The beauty of the Hawaiian quilt has always been the echo quilting. The wave-like ripples that reach out to the edge of the quilt represents Hawai'i's love being sent out to all corners of the world.*

Mahiole
HAWAIIAN WARRIOR'S HELMET

APPLIQUÉD AND QUILTED BY Tomoko Kato, Tokyo, Japan
PERSONAL DESIGN BY John Serrao

45" x 45" Reverse Appliqué

TIME STANDS STILL ON A HAWAIIAN QUILT, A REFLECTION of an era when warriors in their mahiole held to the laws of the land, the people, and the chiefs. *Many quilters believe that quilts made with the theme of the Hawaiian warriors convey strength and power.*

Nā Koa ʻUhane O Hawaiʻi
THE SPIRIT WARRIORS OF HAWAIʻI

APPLIQUÉD AND QUILTED BY Kaori Kaneshiro, Honolulu, Hawaiʻi
PERSONAL DESIGN BY John Serrao

45" x 45" Reverse Appliqué

SOME QUILT DESIGNS ARE REMINISCENT OF OLD HAWAIʻI. THE legendary and fierce Hawaiian warriors with their helmets and spears are a popular design for baby quilts, especially for boys: the strength of a warrior, a guardian of truth, and compassion for one another. *This quilt was made using the reverse appliqué to show the spirit warriors hiding in the shadows.*

King Kamehameha I
ALI'I SERIES

APPLIQUÉD AND QUILTED BY Doris Shibuya, Honolulu, Hawai'i
PERSONAL DESIGN BY John Serrao
90" x 90"

MANY CONTEMPORARY HAWAIIAN QUILTS ARE MADE IN HONOR OF LOVED ONES, HISTORIC FIGURES, and Hawai'i's cherished rulers. King Kamehameha I was the first ruling king of a unified Hawai'i, and this quilt depicts his Hawaiian feathered cape and warrior helmet as well as his legendary broken paddle. *Many mainland quilt exhibitions frown upon the bright colors of the Hawaiian quilts. They seem to forget that using bright color fabrics is part of the Hawaiian quilt tradition and appropriate for a quilt made in honor of King Kamehameha the Great.*

Na Mea O Nā Aliʻi

THE SYMBOLS OF HAWAIʻI'S RULERS: THE KĀHILI AND CROWN

APPLIQUÉD AND QUILTED BY Susie Sugi, Tokyo, Japan
COMMERCIAL DESIGN BY John Serrao
60" x 90"

THE KĀHILI SYMBOLIZES THE OLD TRADITIONS OF THE ISLANDS, and the crown, a new ruling structure that eventually led to the loss of an ancient culture. *The art of Hawaiian quilting went dormant during the war years and renaissance around the early 1960s. During its resurgence, many of the designs still reflected old Hawaiʻi and its traditions.*

Ka Māmalahoe Kānāwai

LEGEND OF THE SPLINTERED PADDLE

APPLIQUÉD AND QUILTED BY Susie Sugi, Tokyo, Japan
COMMERCIAL DESIGN BY John Serrao
60" x 90"

BEFORE KAMEHAMEHA BECAME KING, HE WAS HIT ON THE HEAD with his own canoe paddle by some village guards during a scuffle because he broke an old law of the land by traveling after the sun had set. When Kamehameha became king he remembered this incident and abolished that law, making it safe for everyone to travel at night without fear of being killed. This new law became known as the Law of the Splintered Paddle. *Everyone who attends Poakalani's quilting classes understands that John has a strict rule about designing birds or anything with wings. He stopped designing them when he noticed that everyone he designed a bird for eventually moved away from the Islands. Well, John may not like birds but birds like him. Look in the corner of this quilt and you'll notice four birds that flew their way into his design.*

Queen Ka`ahumanu
ALI`I SERIES

APPLIQUÉD AND QUILTED BY Phyllis Hirata, Honolulu, Hawai`i
PERSONAL DESIGN BY John Serrao
108" x 108"

QUEEN KAʻAHUMANU RULED ALONG SIDE HER HUSBAND, KING KAMEHAMEHA I, AND TWO SONS, KAMEHAMEHA II and III. She fought for the rights of women by defying the restriction of women eating with men when she sat down to have a meal with her sons. She would then go on to change the course of history on the Islands when she allowed the missionaries to enter Hawaiʻi. Her most defying act was when she abolished the old religions and traditions of her people, including the hula. This quilt documents the Queen's symbols of old Hawaiʻi: the royal kāhili, warrior helmet, and lei niho palaoa. Quilted on top of the tabu stick in the corner of the quilt is a Christian cross to show her role in a new Hawaiʻi. *Black is not an easy color to appliqué and quilt but sometimes the story behind the quilt influences the color of the quilt with black representing upheaval and change.*

Nānā I Ke Ku`uipo
LOOKING FOR A HUSBAND

APPLIQUÉD AND QUILTED BY Arisa Okano, Honolulu, Hawai`i
COMMERCIAL CENTER DESIGN AND PERSONAL LEI DESIGN BY John Serrao
45" x 45"

THE NAME OF A QUILT CAN CHANGE OVER THE COURSE of it being made. The original name of this quilt was Na Koa, the guardian, but it was being made during the time Arisa decided to settle down, find a husband, and start a family. So she renamed her quilt, "Looking For a Husband." *Some quilts are made with borders or what we call lei. For many Hawaiians it represented their circle of life, never ending and continuous even after death.*

Na Mele O Hawai`i
THE MUSIC OF HAWAII

APPLIQUÉD AND QUILTED BY
Yoshimi Suzuki, Yokohama, Japan
PERSONAL DESIGN BY John Serrao
45" x 45"

THE HAWAIIANS HAD NO WRITTEN LANGUAGE AND many of their stories were memorized and retold in the poetic language of the hula. It was chanted by the rhythm of the pahu and beat of the ipu, and today it is sung to the strum of the 'ukulele. This quilt tells the story of that universal language of song. *The Hawaiians believe there are gateways to the spiritual world where the spirits travel back and forth to help their families in times of need. So many quilt designers purposely drew an open center on their quilts as a gateway for their spiritual families.*

Kamehameha III
Ali`i Series

APPLIQUÉD AND QUILTED BY Tamako Ho, Waipahu, Hawai`i
PERSONAL DESIGN BY John Serrao
90" x 90"

THE CHRONICLE OF KING KAMEHAMEHA III AND THE MAHELE IS TOLD THROUGH THE STITCHES
of this quilt. The eight erupting volcanoes represent the eight islands of Hawai`i being
divided for private ownership. Erupting from the volcanoes, the laua`e plant represents a new
way of life for the Hawaiian people while the center of the quilt showcases Hawai`i's Coat
of Arms. *When Tamako saw this color fabric she knew this would be the only color that would
give this pattern its true meaning. Unfortunately, there wasn't enough fabric to complete the quilt.
She called the textile distributor and sent her son to Los Angeles to purchase the whole
bolt of fabric. The designer may create the design but the quilter completes the story.*

Pōpoki ʻOkika
CAT ORCHIDS

APPLIQUÉD AND QUILTED BY Takako Jenkins, Honolulu, Hawaiʻi
PERSONAL DESIGN BY John Serrao

90" x 90"

THE TALE OF HAWAIʻI IS NOT COMPLETE UNLESS IT INCLUDES COCONUT TREES AND FRAGRANT ORCHIDS.

*We always encourage our quilters to have an idea for their next pattern before they ask John to create
a design. Takako asked John for a large-size pattern for her next project but wasn't sure what
she wanted so John took pencil to paper and started to design this orchid and coconut tree pattern.
When Takako asked what inspired him to make this design, he said that his daughter's cat
ate all his orchids that very morning.*

King Kalākaua
ALI`I SERIES

APPLIQUÉD AND QUILTED BY Tia Waxman, Honolulu, Hawai`i
PERSONAL DESIGN BY John Serrao

90" x 90"

PHOTOGRAPHS, JOURNALS, AND EVEN HAWAIIAN QUILTS CAN RECORD THE MEMORIES OF GREAT leaders and kings. King David Kalākaua, also known as the Merry Monarch, was the second elected king of Hawai`i. His greatest contribution to his people was allowing them to once again sing and dance to the music of old. Soon everyone was dancing to the sacred beat of the pahu and ipu while keeping time with the rattle of the `ulī`ulī. He was also the first king to travel around the world. This quilt of music and stars tells of his travels and great legacy to his people. *By creating designs that document Hawai`i's history, our quilters are fast becoming Hawaiian historians.*

Queen Lili`uokalani
ALI`I SERIES

APPLIQUÉD AND QUILTED BY Hiroko Vaughan, Honolulu, Hawai`i
PERSONAL DESIGN BY John Serrao

90" x 90"

QUEEN LILI`UOKALANI, THE LAST REIGNING MONARCH OF HAWAI`I, RULED HER PEOPLE IN SADNESS. THIS quilt tells of her imprisonment on the `Iolani Palace grounds as well as her talent for music. *Representing the queen's imprisonment, the border of this quilt is the exact design of the gates surrounding the grounds of the `Iolani Palace. Her favorite crown flower at the center of the quilt shows her love for her people, and carefully sewn into the quilt are the words "Aloha `Oe"…the beginning of a famous song she wrote.*

Kanikapila
LET'S PLAY MUSIC

APPLIQUÉD AND QUILTED BY Tamako Ho, for her son Michael. Waipahu, Hawai`i
PERSONAL DESIGN BY John Serrao

90" x 90"

SOMETIMES A QUILT REFLECTS THE DESIRES OF NOT ONLY THE QUILTER BUT ALSO THE RECIPIENT
of the quilt. Tamako's son loves Hawaiian music and this quilt was designed for him
to show both the modern and traditional musical instruments of the Islands, from the
traditional hula instruments of the pahu drum, ipu, and ʻulīʻulī to the modern ʻukulele.

*The Hawaiian quilt is cut from a single piece of material to signify the purity
of the spirit and the unbroken bloodline.*

Monsterra

APPLIQUÉD AND QUILTED BY Mie Morimoto, Tokyo, Japan
PERSONAL DESIGN BY John Serrao
90" x 90"

THE MANY SHADES OF GREEN ARE SEEN THROUGHOUT HAWAI'I'S LANDSCAPE. THE MONSTERRA plant with its large leaves graces many island homes and has also become a popular design in many Hawaiian quilts. *All of our students learn to quilt without the use of tracing pencils. We believe that the spirit guides the hand, and with enough confidence the quilter is able to see the quilting lines.*

Hawaiian Island Sampler

APPLIQUÉD AND QUILTED BY Junko Haba, Honolulu, Hawai'i
PERSONAL DESIGN BY John Serrao

90" x 90"

THIS QUILT CELEBRATES ALL THE ISLANDS OF HAWAI'I. EACH BLOCK REPRESENTS A PARTICULAR ISLAND flower and color: O'ahu ('Ilima—Yellow); Maui (Rose—Pink); Ni'ihau (Shell—White); Kaho'olawe (Hinahina—Gray); State Flower(Yellow—Hibiscus); Kaua'i (Mokihana—Purple); Hawai'i (Lehua—Red); Moloka'i (Kukui Nut—Green); Lāna'i (Kauna'oa—Orange). *Some quilters prefer to make smaller individual squares and then join them together to complete their quilting story.*

Pua Melia

APPLIQUÉD AND QUILTED BY Eriko Furukawa, Niigata, Japan
COMMERCIAL DESIGN BY John Serrao

60" x 90"

THE PLUMERIA IS KNOWN AS HAWAI'I'S LEI FLOWER. MANY QUILTERS CAN RECALL ITS MANY varieties and colors being sewn for hula dancers and lei greeters. *The plumeria will always be one of Hawai'i's favorite flowers and for three friends it will bind their friendship forever. Eriko chose this pattern because she loved the design (as well as the easy appliqué lines) with its long leaves and stems.*

Nā Pua Onaona
SCENTED BLOSSOMS

APPLIQUÉD AND QUILTED BY Yuko Nishiwaki, Kobe, Japan
COMMERCIAL CENTER DESIGN AND PERSONAL LEI DESIGN BY John Serrao

90" x 90"

THE PLUMERIA CAN BE FOUND THROUGHOUT THE PACIFIC ISLANDS. ALSO KNOWN AS THE FRANGIPANI, ITS strong scent is widely used in shampoos, perfumes, and potpourri. *Yuko also chose a commercial plumeria design but decided to add a free-floating border. Her color choice of pink was her granddaughter's suggestion.*

Lei Pua Melia

APPLIQUÉD AND QUILTED BY Sanae Fuchisawa, Honolulu, Hawai`i
COMMERCIAL CENTER DESIGN AND PERSONAL LEI DESIGN BY John Serrao
90" x 90"

IN HAWAI'I THE PLUMERIA IS ALSO KNOWN AS THE "DEAD MAN'S FLOWER" BECAUSE IT CAN
always be found growing in Hawai'i's cemeteries. *Sanae's first single-bed quilt was a
commercial plumeria design. To make it unique she decided to add a border design. Sanae, Yuko,
and Eriko met in one of the quilting classes and became close friends but it wasn't until they
displayed their quilts in an exhibit that they discovered they quilted the same
plumeria center design, a sign for them that their friendship was destined.*

Nā Pali O Koʻolau
THE CLIFFS OF THE KOOLAU

APPLIQUÉD AND QUILTED BY Lynette Yee, Honolulu, Hawaiʻi
PERSONAL DESIGN BY John Serrao

60" x 90"

THE MONSTERRA PLANT GROWS WILD IN THE NATURAL FOREST ALONG THE CLIFFS OF THE KOʻOLAU. *Choosing a quilt design can be very difficult. For some it comes in a dream. For others it's a personal desire. For Lynette it's all about large leaves and easy appliqué. Lynette told us how she was waiting in line at a drive-through restaurant when she noticed the Monsterra plant growing around its perimeter. All she saw were HUGE Monsterra leaves and decided that would be her next design.*

Bird of Paradise

APPLIQUÉD AND QUILTED BY Wilma Makilan, Pearl City, Hawai'i
COMMERCIAL CENTER DESIGN AND PERSONAL BORDER DESIGN BY John Serrao

60" x 90"

QUILTS ARE NOT JUST ABOUT THE DESIGN OR THE STORY BUT ALSO ABOUT FUNCTIONALITY. Many homes in Hawai'i are getting smaller, so quilters are making smaller quilts for the twin-size bed. By still using a 1/4 symmetrical fold instead of the 1/8 fold, the quilt becomes more rectangle than square. *Many quilters are accenting their echo quilting by quilting Hawaiian motifs in sections of the quilt to add a new feature to their quilt.*

Pikapua O Pu`uwai
FLOWERS OF MY HEART

APPLIQUÉD AND QUILTED BY Tomiko Okada, Kobe, Japan
PERSONAL DESIGN BY John Serrao
90" x 90"

THE HELICONIA SEEN IN VASES OR GROWING WILD HAS ALWAYS BEEN A PERSONAL FAVORITE OF
Tomiko, so she wanted to capture the flower on a Hawaiian quilt. *Which do you enjoy
more, appliqué or quilting? When choosing a design we always tell our quilters, if the design
is very intricate, you'll be spending most of your time appliquéing and less time quilting.*

Honu ʻAukai
THE OCEAN TRAVELLER

APPLIQUÉD AND QUILTED BY
Tomoko Kato, Tokyo, Japan
PERSONAL DESIGN BY John Serrao
45" x 60"

TRADITIONS IN HAWAIʻI WERE SOMETIMES A CONTRADICTION to each other. The green sea turtles lived in Hawaiʻi even before the first settlers. When the natives arrived they worshiped them as spirit guardians while others viewed them as a food source. *Like the turtles, Hawaiian quilts live on through several generations.*

Iʻa O Ke Kai
FISH OF THE SEA

APPLIQUÉD AND QUILTED BY Takako Jinushi, Tokyo, Japan
PERSONAL DESIGN BY John Serrao
45" x 60"

IN THE EARLY DAYS OF HAWAIIAN QUILTING, FLOWERS WERE the main design for quilts. Today, with the ocean on our door step, the theme of fishes, dolphins, and sea life has gained popularity. *All quilting classes go through phases. Ours went through an ocean phase when all the patterns being made were about dolphins, fish, and sea life.*

Liliko`i

APPLIQUÉD AND QUILTED BY Ale Hogue, La Habra, California
Caroline Correa Vintage Quilt Collection circa 1920
90" x 90"

CHILDREN NEVER WENT HUNGRY IN THE ISLANDS BECAUSE A TYPICAL HAWAIIAN YARD GREW A variety of plants and fruit trees especially mangoes, lychee, guava, mountain apples, avocados, star fruit, and Hawai'i's passion fruit—the liliko'i. *The majority of Hawaiian quilts are made squared because the medallion design is symmetrically squared. However, by using a longer background fabric the quilt can be adjusted to fit longer beds.*

Tokiko's Mele
TOKIKO'S SONG

APPLIQUÉD AND QUILTED BY
Tokiko Furukawa, Honolulu, Hawai`i
PERSONAL DESIGN BY John Serrao
45" x 60"

IN HAWAI'I IT'S ALWAYS ABOUT THE MUSIC AND THE DANCE OF the Islands. *Many quilters are breaking away from the traditional solid colors of a Hawaiian quilt and are now using batiks and other printed fabric. While the quilt is still a traditional design the colors give it a more contemporary look.*

Ti Leaf

APPLIQUÉD AND QUILTED BY
Yoko Niizawa, Honolulu, Hawai`i
PERSONAL DESIGN BY John Serrao
45" x 60"

THE TI LEAF IS HAWAI'I'S MOST CHERISHED PLANT. IT WAS used for cooking and medicine and planted around the house to bring good luck as well as ward off evil spirits. *Today many quilters are making this pattern and placing it at the front entrance of their home for protection.*

Na Ali`i O `Awapuhi

APPLIQUÉD AND QUILTED BY Mie Morimoto, Tokyo, Japan
PERSONAL DESIGN BY John Serrao

90" x 90"

NATIVE TO INDIA, THE KĀHILI GINGER EVENTUALLY FOUND A HOME IN HAWAI`I'S DENSE FORESTS. THE
fragrant yellow flowers that grow from a center stem closely resemble Hawai`i's own royal standards.
Mie wanted a quilt that would convey her love for the ginger flower and Hawai`i, so John designed a quilt
to reflect both desires. He fashioned the kāhili ginger to look like Hawai`i's precious royal kāhili.

Mele Kalikimaka

MERRY CHRISTMAS

APPLIQUÉD AND QUILTED BY
Yuko Nishiwaki, Kobe, Japan
PERSONAL DESIGN BY John Serrao
45" x 45"

THE INTERNATIONAL TRADITION OF HANGING a Christmas wreath is also popular in Hawai'i but Christmas in the Islands is blessed with sun, surf, cool breezes, and no snow. *In 1862, Christmas became an official holiday in Hawai'i.*

Kukui 'Ohana O Cecile

THE LIGHT OF CECILE'S FAMILY

APPLIQUÉD AND QUILTED BY
Cecile Medeiros, Kailua, Hawai'i
PERSONAL DESIGN BY John Serrao
45" x 60"

THE LANTERN ILIMA FLOWER IS SEEN MOSTLY IN FLORAL LEI BUT the kaona or hidden meaning on this quilt speaks of that inner light that guides one's family. *Quilting or appliqué? When the pattern is simple, there is always less appliqué and more quilting.*

ʻUlu

APPLIQUÉD AND QUILTED BY
Colleen Holmes, Kaneohe, Hawaiʻi
COMMERCIAL DESIGN BY John Serrao
45" x 45"

THE ʻULU OR BREADFRUIT HAS COME TO SYMBOLIZE abundance and bountifulness in money, food, and family. That is why some quilters will make this quilt design first for themselves, special family, and friends. *Hawaiian quilting teaches patience. It centers and focuses you after a long day at work.*

Na Koa
THE GUARDIAN

APPLIQUÉ AND QUILTED BY
Colleen Holmes, Kaneohe, Hawaiʻi
COMMERCIAL DESIGN BY John Serrao
45" x 45"

NA KOA WERE THE WARRIORS OF HAWAIʻI. They protected the people and their land and we believe our quilters are the Na Koa of their family. *This design incorporates the warrior's helmet, spear, and war club.*

Hilo Hanakahi

APPLIQUÉD AND QUILTED BY Kaori Kaneshiro, Honolulu, Hawai'i
Caroline Correa Vintage Quilt Collection circa 1920
90" x 90"

HILO IS ONE OF THE MOST BEAUTIFUL TOWNS IN THE STATE OF HAWAI'I—
from the beautiful lehua blossoms of the Pana'ewa Forest to the people who give this town its aloha.
*We tell all our quilters to always label their quilts. The name of the design, the year it
was completed, who it was designed for, who quilted it, and the meaning of the quilt.
It's the quilter's signature that completes the story to the quilt.*

Hilo Beauty

APPLIQUÉD AND QUILTED BY Yuki Orikasa, Tokyo, Japan
Caroline Correa Vintage Quilt Collection circa 1920
108" x 108"

MANY VINTAGE QUILTS WERE DESIGNED IN HONOR OF A QUILTER'S HOME. THIS QUILT,
Hilo Beauty, speaks of love for that special place. *Many vintage quilts were designed
with smaller medallion centers on a larger fabric backing so the center of the design fit
perfectly on the middle of the bed while the wide borders draped down its side.*

The Garden of Aloha

LILI'UOKALANI'S WASHINGTON PLACE

APPLIQUÉD AND QUILTED BY
June Gerber, Belton, Texas
PERSONAL DESIGN BY June Gerber

45" x 60"

AFTER READING QUEEN LILI'UOKALANI'S BOOK, *Hawai'i's Story by Hawai'i's Queen,* June wanted a quilt depicting the queen's gardens. The spider lily, banana trees, and her favorite crown flower are incorporated into the quilt design. Also sewn into the quilt are the queen and her royal symbols. *June is an award-winning quilter and designer. Her patterns are a combination of quilt design and definitive quilting, accenting each other to tell the story.*

Kukui Ula Hale 'O Queen Emma

THE LIGHTS OF QUEEN EMMA

APPLIQUÉD AND QUILTED BY
June Gerber, Belton, Texas
PERSONAL DESIGN BY June Gerber

45" x 60"

INCORPORATING DIFFERENT DECORATIVE stitches within a Hawaiian quilt border, June was able to depict the Queen Emma Summer Palace in Nu'uanu Valley. The queen stands in the doorway looking out at the old-fashioned lanterns lighting the driveway. *Some quilt patterns are designed using the 1/2 fold because it gives the quilt designer more space for artistic expression.*

Kumula`au Niu

APPLIQUÉD AND QUILTED BY Anne-Marie Norton, Honolulu, Hawai`i
PERSONAL DESIGN BY John Serrao

60" x 90"

THE BEAUTY OF THE HAWAIIAN QUILT CAN ALSO BE SEEN IN THE CONTINUOUS LINE OF THE ECHO
quilting that graces the edges of the quilt. A simple design of coconut trees and laua`e
is given movement by the echo quilting. *It takes thousands of stitches to create a quilt.*
That's why we believe the greatest gift you can receive is a Hawaiian quilt.

Tropical Hawai'i

APPLIQUÉD AND QUILTED BY
Mie Morimoto, Tokyo, Japan
PERSONAL DESIGN BY Mie Morimoto
45" x 60" Reverse Appliqué

WHILE MOST QUILTS ARE JUST ONE SINGLE design, reverse quilts can portray multiple motifs. This quilt talks about the beauty of Hawai'i through the hibiscus, laua'e, dolphins, ocean waves, orchids, and coconut trees. *Reverse appliqué is exciting to make. While appliquéing, each design appears like magic, revealing the secrets of the quilt.*

Turtles & Dolphins

APPLIQUÉD AND QUILTED BY
Yoshimi Suzuki, Yokohama, Japan
PERSONAL DESIGN BY Yoshimi Suzuki
45" x 45"

HAWAI'I IS KNOWN FOR ITS OCEAN REEFS THAT are a kaleidoscope of colorful sea life. This quilt represents our wonderful creatures of the sea. *Some fabric color creates an illusion on the quilt where the design is hidden behind a myriad of color.*

Tropical Paradise

APPLIQUÉD AND QUILTED BY Ale Hogue, La Habra, California
COMMERCIAL DESIGNS BY John Serrao,
"Poakalani Hawaiian Cushion Patterns Volume I & II"
90" x 108"

HAWAI'I IS A TROPICAL GARDEN. WHETHER YOU'RE IN THE CITY OR COUNTRY, FLOWERS BLOOM on street corners, narrow roads, and even the freeways. This quilt expresses Hawai'i's love for flowers and gardens. *An expert in all forms of quilting, Ale also has an eye for color as well as design placement. If done correctly, the colors of the quilt will showcase each design without overpowering each other.*

Pua Nui O Ka Punahou
NIGHT BLOOMING CEREUS

APPLIQUÉD AND QUILTED BY Tia Waxman for her daughter Teppi, Honolulu, Hawai`i
PERSONAL DESIGN BY John Serrao

108" x 108"

PART OF THE CACTI FAMILY, THE NIGHT BLOOMING CEREUS GROWS WILD ON THE GROUNDS OF Punahou School. Blooming only at night once a year, the large, white scented flower has become one of the school's main attractions. *Tia's daughter graduated from Punahou School. She wanted a design for her daughter that would have a special meaning, so she chose the Night Blooming Cereus.*

ʻEhu Kai
THE SEA

APPLIQUED AND QUILTED BY Wilma Makilan, Pearl City, Hawaiʻi
PERSONAL DESIGN BY John Serrao

90" x 90"

TOURISTS COME FROM ALL OVER THE WORLD TO RELAX, PLAY, AND SWIM AT HAWAIʻI'S BEACHES, but for many local people the ocean is their life source. It feeds their family and cleanses their soul. *Everyone enjoys watching a quilter slowly open their design from its 1/8 fold to its full design revealing the quilt's secret. For Wilma, it was forty-eight turtles, eight dolphins, and four octopus.*

Bombax

APPLIQUÉD AND QUILTED BY Tia Waxman, for her granddaughter Makena, Honolulu, Hawai`i
PERSONAL DESIGN BY John Serrao
108" x 108"

POAKALANI'S QUILTING CLASSES WERE ONCE HELD AT THE QUEEN EMMA SUMMER PALACE
in Nuʻuanu. Landscaped with tropical flowers and Hawaiian foliage, the Bombax tree greeted
quilters as they entered the driveway leading to the palace. *It takes thousands of stitches to
complete a Hawaiian quilt—that's why it's called a labor of love .*

Plumeria

APPLIQUÉD AND QUILTED BY Yukie Orikasa, Tokyo, Japan
PERSONAL DESIGN BY John Serrao

90" x 90"

ONE OF THE MOST FRAGRANT FLOWER IN HAWAIʻI IS THE PLUMERIA BLOSSOMS USED IN FLORAL arrangements, lei, and island decorations. *You don't have to live in Hawaiʻi to be a Hawaiian quilter. You don't even have to be Hawaiian to be a Hawaiian quilter. A Hawaiian quilter is someone who quilts in the traditional style of Hawaiʻi: folding the fabric in a symmetrical fold, cutting out the design in one piece, hand appliquéing as well as hand quilting, and most of all, telling their story in the quilt. Yuki teaches Hawaiian quilting in Tokyo, Japan. She not only teaches the basic sewing techniques but she also shares with her class the traditions and people of Hawaiʻi. Hawaiian quilting is for everyone.*

Anthurium

APPLIQUÉD AND QUILTED BY Tamako Ho, for her granddaughter Dana, Waipahu, Hawai`i
PERSONAL DESIGN BY John Serrao

108" x 108"

ANTHURIUMS ARE ONE OF HAWAI`I'S FAVORITE FLOWERS BECAUSE OF THEIR LARGE VARIETIES OF COLORS, shapes, and sizes but most of all for the flower's heart-shaped leaves that always convey a message of love. *Some people believe that making a quilt with more than three colors is bad luck. We believe that a quilt made with love and given with love can only bring happiness to everyone who is part of the quilt.*

ʻŪlei Berries

APPLIQUÉD AND QUILTED BY Tomoko Kato, Tokyo, Japan
Caroline Correa Vintage Quilt Collection circa 1920
90" x 90"

A POPULAR VINTAGE QUILT DESIGN, THE ʻŪLEI BERRY IS FROM A WOODY SHRUB KNOWN FOR ITS SMALL white flowers and white fruit. The Hawaiians also used the wood to make fishing spears and digging sticks. *Because of the lack of fabric, many vintage Hawaiian quilts were made with solid colors, mainly with a dark design on a light backing. Today, with a larger selection of fabrics, many of the vintage quilt patterns are being reborn with a more contemporary look. Tomoko teaches quilting in Tokyo, Japan. She is not only an excellent quilt instructor but she has a unique talent for combining color.*

African Tulip

APPLIQUÉD AND QUILTED BY Susie Sugi, Tokyo, Japan
PERSONAL DESIGN BY John Serrao

90" x 90"

WITH THE INTRODUCTION OF NEW PLANTS AND FLOWERS TO THE ISLANDS, NEW HAWAIIAN QUILT
patterns have began to appear. Today, the island of Oʻahu has a large abundance of
African Tulip trees. Their bright red flowers add a new shade of color to the greenery
that surrounds the mountains and valleys. *The local kids have a special fondness for this
tree because the center of the flower holds buds that squirt water when squeezed.*

Pua Ku`uipo

APPLIQUÉD AND QUILTED BY Noriko Bartek, Kailua, Hawai`i
COMMERCIAL CENTER AND PERSONAL BORDER DESIGN BY John Serrao

108" x 108"

THIS DESIGN CAPTURES THE BEAUTY OF THE ANTHURIUM FLOWER, WHICH GROWS IN A VARIETY
of different colors. *Some quilters like to expand a smaller full-size quilt design into the larger
king-size pattern. This is simply done by purchasing fabric for the larger quilt. Just place the
smaller quilt pattern on the fabric then design a new border on its edge.*

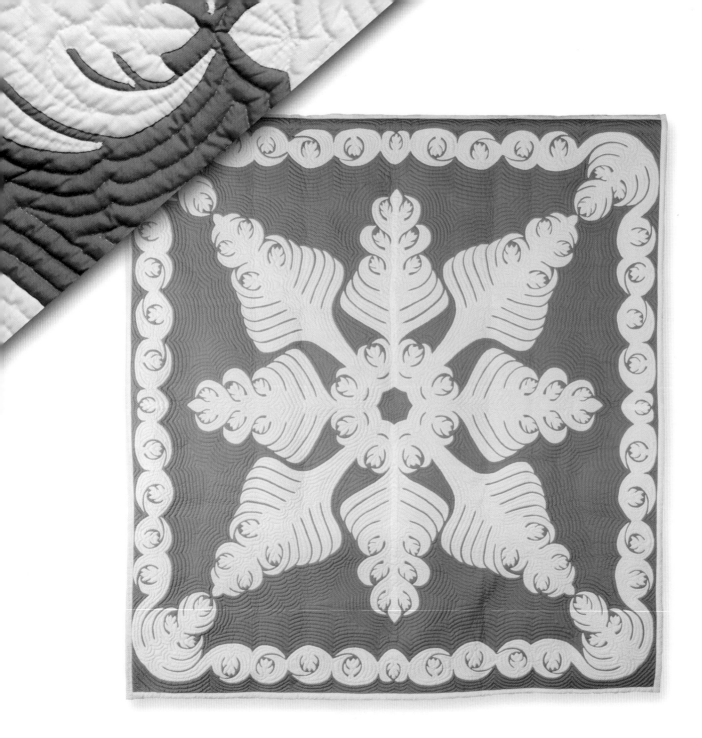

Silversword

APPLIQUÉD AND QUILTED BY Tamako Ho, Waipahu, Hawai`i
PERSONAL DESIGN BY John Serrao

90" x 90"

TAMAKO ALWAYS LOVED THE SILVERSWORD AND WANTED TO CAPTURE ITS RARE BEAUTY ONTO a Hawaiian quilt. She took a trip to Maui and drove up to the slopes of Haleakalā to see the silversword in its natural environment. This quilt is a reflection of what she saw on her trip. *When your design is inspired by an inner desire, the result is a masterpiece of color and design.*

Kaomi Mālie

APPLIQUÉD AND QUILTED BY Arisa Okano, Honolulu, Hawai`i
Caroline Correa Vintage Quilt Collection circa 1890
90" x 90"

THIS QUILT WAS DESIGNED BY A WIFE WHO WOULD GENTLY MASSAGE HER HUSBAND'S ACHES AND PAINS away after a hard day at work. While making this quilt Arisa met her husband and gave this quilt a second name called "Found A Husband." *The older vintage-quilt designers usually designed their quilts on the bias and straight of their fabric with the branches of the design reaching out from the center.*

Anthurium

APPLIQUÉD AND QUILTED BY Tomiko Okada
COMMERCIAL DESIGN BY John Serrao

45" x 45"

THE HEART-SHAPED LEAVES OF THE ANTHURIUM always make it a favorite design for weddings, but you can create your own quilt story by sewing this pattern, found on page 86.

Taro

APPLIQUÉD AND QUILTED BY
Kimi Kumagai, Nagoya, Japan
COMMERCIAL DESIGN BY John Serrao

45" x 45"

THE TARO DESIGN HAS ALWAYS SYMBOLIZED family in Hawai'i, but you can create your own quilt story by sewing this pattern, found on page 87.

Hearts & Roses

APPLIQUÉD AND QUILTED BY
Keiko Sakamoto, Honolulu, Hawai`i
COMMERCIAL DESIGN BY John Serrao
45" x 45"

HEARTS & ROSES CONVEY MANY MESSAGES OF love, but you can create your own quilt story by sewing this pattern, found on page 89.

Star Plumeria

APPLIQUÉD AND QUILTED BY
Tomoko Kato, Tokyo, Japan
COMMERCIAL DESIGN BY John Serrao
45" x 45"

THE STAR-SHAPED FLOWERS OF THE plumeria can convey many meanings, but you can create your own quilt story by sewing this pattern, found on page 88.

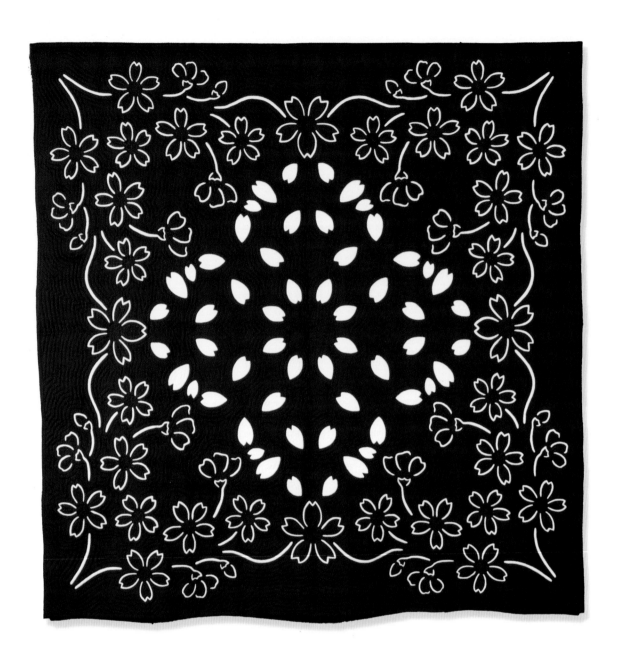

Sakura

APPLIQUÉD AND QUILTED BY Kimi Kumagai, Nagoya, Japan
PERSONAL DESIGN BY Kimi Kumagai
90" x 90" Reverse Applique

CHERRY BLOSSOMS BLOOM ONCE A YEAR AND FOR ONLY TWO WEEKS, WITH MANY FESTIVALS BEGINNING
at the flowers' first bloom lasting through to their lovely showers. However, the cherry blossoms
on this quilt bloom throughout the year. *Kimi teaches Hawaiian quilting in Nagoya, Japan.*
She has been able to learn the fine and intricate stitches of Hawaiian quilting and also the
creative technique of designing her own patterns.

He Pule Kākou
LET US PRAY

APPLIQUÉD AND QUILTED BY
Junko Haba, Honolulu, Hawai`i
PERSONAL DESIGN BY Junko Haba
45" x 45"

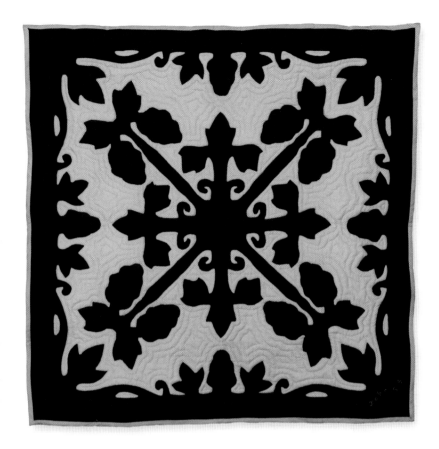

JOHN 15:5 I AM THE VINE, YE ARE THE
branches: ye that abideth in me, and I in
him, the same bringeth forth much fruit: for
without me ye can do nothing. *The
"WORD" is spoken in many languages,
celebrated in art, song, and dance, and
now interpreted on a Hawaiian quilt and
rejoicing in one's own baptism.*

Loke Lani
HEAVENLY ROSE

APPLIQUÉD AND QUILTED BY
Lily Kobayashi, Honolulu, Hawai`i
PERSONAL DESIGN BY John Serrao
45" x 45"

THE LOKE LANI BLOSSOMS WAS A FAVORITE VARIETY
of roses of Queen Emma. *All our quilters start off
with a 22" x 22" cushion pattern. At this beginning
stage they're learning the basics of basting,
appliquéing, quilting, and refining their stitches.
Their next step is usually the 45" x 45" design,
at which stage their quilting has already been
perfected—they're more relaxed in their sewing and
starting to fully enjoy the art of Hawaiian quilting.*

Bird of Paradise

APPLIQUÉD AND QUILTED BY Toshie Takashima, Osaka, Japan
COMMERCIAL CENTER DESIGN AND PERSONAL BORDER DESIGN BY John Serrao
90" x 90"

THE BIRD OF PARADISE IS A NATIVE OF SOUTH AFRICA BUT HAS FOUND A SECOND HOME IN HAWAI'I. Its long stem and bird-shaped flowers makes it popular for home landscaping and tropical arrangements. *Through creative designing, this quilt was made by using a 45" x 45"commercial pattern for its center and then adding a newly-designed border.*

Ku'u Home Me Kela 'Ao'Ao
MY HOME ACROSS THE SEA

APPLIQUÉD AND QUILTED BY Tomiko Okada, Kobe, Japan
PERSONAL DESIGN BY Tomiko Okada

60" x 90"

HAWAIIAN QUILTS ARE SNAPSHOTS INTO THE HEARTS OF QUILTERS. ASK TOMIKO WHAT REMINDS her of Hawai'i and she'll tell you—banana trees, pineapples, and laua'e. *John was the first designer to conduct design workshops in Hawai'i. He wanted to be sure that the art of designing would be passed on to a new generation of quilters. Today, many of our students are not only quilting but designing their own quilting legacy.*

Monsterra

APPLIQUÉD AND QUILTED BY Wilma Makilan, Pearl City, Hawai`i
PERSONAL DESIGN BY John Serrao

90" x 90"

PERSONALLY DESIGNED FOR WILMA, THIS MONSTERRA QUILT WAS ONE OF THE FIRST LARGE PIECES she completed. She will tell you how she loved quilting the large Monsterra leaves but those little holes on the leaf will test any great appliquér. *Our quilt exhibitions are always unique; all the quilts showcased are one-of-a-kind. Some of the quilts may have a similar theme but every design is exclusive to the individual quilter.*

Hibiscus

APPLIQUÉD AND QUILTED BY Anne-Marie Norton, Honolulu, Hawai`i
DESIGNED BY John Serrao
90" x 90"

THE HIBISCUS WILL ALWAYS BE A FAVORITE DESIGN AMONG HAWAI`I'S QUILTERS. ITS LARGE
distinctive flowers and long stems make it especially easy for the beginner quilter. *The very middle
of a Hawaiian quilt design is called its center. The center is always quilted first because it is the focal
point of the quilt, and it is believed to be the center of the quilter, the life force and life energy.*

Shower Tree

APPLIQUÉD AND QUILTED BY Takako Jenkins, Honolulu, Hawai`i
PERSONAL DESIGN BY Takako Jenkins

90" x 90"

SHOWER TREES LINE THE MANY FREEWAYS AND ROADS OF HONOLULU. THEIR COLORS VARY FROM soft pinks to bright yellows. *Takako created this pattern in one of John's quilt design workshops. She learned to create quilt patterns starting with only a blank sheet of paper and no stencils, just her hearts' desire and artistic ability. Now her tradition and spiritual legacy will be passed on forever.*

Orchids

APPLIQUÉD AND QUILTED BY Yoshimi Suzuki, Yokohama, Japan
PERSONAL DESIGN BY John Serrao
90" x 90"

BREAKING AWAY FROM THE TRADITIONAL TWO-COLOR QUILTS, MANY QUILTERS ARE NOW ADDING
multi-layered colors to their designs, a new concept in Hawaiian quilting. However, be careful
since you will be quilting through five layers of fabric and batting. *In order for our traditions
to survive, they must be taught and passed on. Yoshimi teaches Hawaiian quilting in
Yokohama, Japan. We teach the students the basics of Hawaiian quilting and designing,
and eventually they are able to pass on that tradition by
teaching classes in their own hometown.*

Kapa Pohopoho

APPLIQUÉD AND QUILTED BY The Holoholo Quilt Club, Tokyo, Japan
COMMERCIAL DESIGNS BY John Serrao, "Hawaiian Cushion Patterns Volume IV"

90" x 90"

SOME SAMPLER QUILTS ARE A COLLECTIVE EXPRESSION OF SEVERAL HAWAIIAN QUILTERS DEDICATED to complete one ambition a Hawaiian quilt. *We always teach our quilters that every quilt they make embodies part of their spirit. A sampler quilt embodies multiple spirits that express unity of mind and heart. This quilt was made by the Holoholo Club, our sister-quilting club in Tokyo, Japan. Their support, enthusiasm, and dedication to the art of Hawaiian quilting perpetuate a Hawaiian tradition worldwide.*

HOLOHOLO QUILT CLUB OF JAPAN MEMBERS:

Mitsue Baba, Mariko Takahashi, Kiyomi Itou, Miyoko Itou,
Chikako Asano, Wakako Shionoya

Monsterra & Gecko

APPLIQUÉD AND QUILTED BY
Nobuko Nakagawa, Osaka, Japan
PERSONAL DESIGN BY Nobuko Nakagawa
45" x 60"

GECKOS ENJOYING THE SUN ON A GARDEN OF MONSTERRA
leaves. *Reverse appliqué was always used to accent Hawaiian
quilts. On this quilt, the Hawaiian geckos appear on each leaf
tanning in the sun.*

Climbing Turtles

APPLIQUÉD AND QUILTED BY
Chiyo Narashima, Honolulu, Hawai`i
PERSONAL DESIGN BY John Serrao
45" x 45"

TURTLES CAN'T REALLY CLIMB TREES, BUT
the love this student has for turtles inspired
the creation of this design. *Chiyo made three
quilts with this design and lovingly gave them
to her family.*

Mele Nai`a
SINGING DOLPHINS

APPLIQUÉD AND QUILTED BY Yuko Nishiwaki, Kobe, Japan
PERSONAL DESIGN BY John Serrao

90" x 90"

THE COLOR OF THE QUILT NEVER CHANGES THE DESIGN. SINGING WHITE DOLPHINS WITH PLUMERIAS
on a red backing reveal the quilter's favorite color. *When choosing to make a quilt with a light
design, the dark backing can sometimes change the color of the top fabric ever so slightly.*

Takako's Goldfish

APPLIQUÉD AND QUILTED BY
Takako Jenkins, Honolulu, Hawai`i
PERSONAL DESIGN BY John Serrao
45" x 45"

MEMORY QUILTS LIKE PHOTOGRAPHS BRING BACK
for the quilters days of long past. Takako always
had goldfishes when she was living in Ohio. Today
her goldfishes are no longer in an aquarium but
on a Hawaiian quilt. *Without a story, quilts are just
blankets on a bed.*

Hibiscus & Griffin

APPLIQUÉD AND QUILTED BY
Hiroko Vaughan, Honolulu, Hawai`i
PERSONAL DESIGN BY John Serrao
45" x 45"

SOME QUILTS CAPTURE TIMELESS EMOTIONS
THAT will live on forever. This quilt tells the
story of a wife's love for her husband. The
hibiscus represents Hiroko's island home
of Hawai`i, while the griffin symbolizes her
husband's ancestral home of Wales. Together
they represent two traditions but one love.
*Incorporating logos, themes, and symbols from
different cultures makes the art of Hawaiian
quilting internationally unique.*

Mele Nai`a

APPLIQUÉD AND QUILTED BY Mitsue Toi, Tokyo, Japan
PERSONAL DESIGN BY John Serrao

90" x 90"

AN OLD LEGEND SPEAKS OF A BEAUTIFUL PRINCESS WHO WAS KIDNAPPED AND TAKEN OUT TO sea by hostile natives. In an attempt to escape her captors, she jumped overboard in the cold ocean water and began to swim back to shore. After swimming for some time she grew weary, and when she felt that she would never see her family again, a school of dolphins came up from below her with their bodies swimming closely together. They slowly lifted her up from the ocean like a raft and swiftly brought her to shore. Her native people and family were grateful to such kind creatures of God and from that day forward protected the dolphins from any harm.

Mitsue wanted a design that reflected her daughter's favorite hobby of scuba diving. The final pattern was 16 dolphins dancing wildly in the tropical blue ocean.

Hula Hula Nai`a
DANCING DOLPHINS

APPLIQUÉD AND QUILTED BY
Yoko Niizawa, Honolulu, Hawai`i
COMMERCIAL DESIGN BY John Serrao

45" x 60"

YOKO LOVES EVERYTHING HAWAIIAN—FROM CRAFTING feather lei to sewing Hawaiian quilts. This dolphin quilt expresses her love for the ocean and its wondrous creatures. *The 45" x 60" quilt patterns were designed to fit inside a baby's crib.*

He`e

APPLIQUÉD AND QUILTED BY Phyllis Hirata, Honolulu, Hawai`i
PERSONAL DESIGN BY John Serrao and Phyllis Hirata
45" x 60"

KOI (FISH) SWIMMING THROUGH THE LEGS OF THE OCTOPUS. *A quilt design is a collaboration of two people—the designer and the quilter. John made the octopus pattern and Phyllis added the koi printed fabric to give the quilt her personal expression. This quilt has become Phyllis' signature quilt. She has already made three for friends and family.*

`Ohana Nai`a
FAMILY OF DOLPHINS

APPLIQUED AND QUILTED BY Keiko Kawai, Kyushu, Japan
PERSONAL DESIGN BY John Serrao

90" x 90"

THIS QUILT REPRESENTS A FAMILY OF DOLPHINS TRAVELING TOGETHER PROTECTING AND NURTURING each other throughout their lives. *Keiko teaches Hawaiian quilting in Kyushu, Japan with the assistance of her artist husband, Isamu. The blending of her quilting style and his attention to detail is truly a Hawaiian tradition of family working hand-in-hand perpetuating one's own legacy.*

King Pineapple

APPLIQUÉD AND QUILTED BY Keiko Nakamura, Tokyo, Japan
Caroline Correa Vintage Quilt Collection circa 1920
90" x 90"

PINEAPPLES ARE INTERNATIONALLY KNOWN AS THE FRIENDSHIP FRUIT BUT IN HAWAIʻI IT WAS
called King Pineapple because it was Hawaiʻi's major commercial industry. *Definitive quilting is
used in many Hawaiian quilts to give the design more detail and expression. The pineapples in this
quilt have those wonderful textured dimples just like a real pineapple.*

Ku`u Hae Owyhee
HAWAI`I'S FLAG

APPLIQUÉD AND QUILTED BY Tomiko Okada, Kobe, Japan
PERSONAL DESIGN BY Tomiko Okada

REPRESENTING SADNESS FOR A LOST KINGDOM, AND PRIDE FOR OUR STATE AND NATIVE PEOPLE, the Hawaiian flag quilts became popular during the overthrow of Hawai`i's kingdom in 1893. *A secret about sewing flag quilts: traditionally, all Hawaiian quilts are done by hand, however with most flag quilts, the stripes on a flag quilt are joined on a sewing machine.*

Beginning Your Masterpiece

We hope that you were so inspired by our quilters' masterpieces that you now have the desire to create your very own quilt. So, in the spirit and tradition of Hawai'i, and from our quilting class to you, we have included patterns and instructions to help you begin your masterpiece.

SUPPLY LIST

Fabric

The best way to decide on fabric is touch and feel. Look for a tight weave but not too tight that you'll have difficulty pushing the needle through, not too loose where the weave will not spring back in place. Lighter fabric is always easier to sew.

cushion 22" x 22"	5/8 yards each for top piece, backing, and quilt backing
wallhanging 45" x 45"	45" each for top piece, backing, and quilt backing
wallhanging 45" x 60"	60" each for top piece, backing, and quilt backing
twin 60" x 90"	Two pieces of fabric: 60" each for top piece, backing, and quilt backing
full & queen 90" x 90"	6 yards each for top piece, backing, and quilt backing
king 108" x 108"	9 yards each for top piece, backing, and quilt backing

cotton	Always the best, and please remember to pre-wash all fabrics, especially if you plan to use different types of fabrics on one quilt.
poly-blends	Another great choice. It's colorfast, and the color will last longer over the years than cotton.
batiks	Great choice for printed fabric that can enhance the quilt design and backing.
aloha prints	Great for quilt backings, but using a solid color on the back of the quilt showcases the quilting stitch which creates a lovely shadow quilt.
cotton sheets	If you can find a flat sheet in your preferred color, but only use sheets with a 180-weave count.

Choice of Fabric Colors

Traditionally, the Hawaiians used a dark solid color on white backing only because those were the only colors available. Then quilts evolved to brighter, bolder colors, and today with the larger choice of fabrics many quilters are using printed and batik fabrics. Darker colors are more difficult to see, more so in the evenings. Also, using a light-on-dark color fabric is becoming popular but be careful on the larger-size quilts; your seams may be more pronounced. Remember, the color of the quilt does not change the design.

Batting

You may want your batting a little larger than the actual quilt size to accommodate any shirking during the quilting process.

cushion	5/8 yards	**wallhanging**	60"	**full & queen**	6 yards
22" x 22"		45" x 60"		90" x 90"	
wallhanging	45"	**twin**	120"	**king**	9 yards
45" x 45"		60" x 90"		108" x 108"	

Most of our quilters use a 5 oz. polyester batting but cotton is another great choice to use. The polyester gives the quilt a more contemporary look. The heavier the batting, the more pronounced the contours of the echo quilting. Cotton batting gives the quilt a more flat, antique look.

Appliqué Pins

Tacks down the top fabric design to the backing fabric for basting

Silk pins are the best. They slide through fabric easily, but they are very expensive and sometimes difficult to find.

Needles

Sharps of various sizes for appliqué; betweens of various sizes for quilting

Sharps are thinner needles mostly used for appliqué; betweens are more sturdy and perfect for quilting. Test-drive the different sizes of your needles until you find the size that you're comfortable with.

Thread

BASTING THREAD: Any unused thread you have at home is great for basting.

APPLIQUÉ THREAD: All-purpose thread is fine. Use the same color as the design but an excellent appliquér can actually use any color thread. Silk thread in brown, beige, or taupe can also be used for any color design.

QUILTING THREAD: Always try to use quilting thread. If unavailable, use the all-purpose thread but just make the thread shorter when quilting. Use the same thread color as the design or back fabric or, if you feel artistic, use a darker or lighter color thread to enhance the quilt. Traditionally, white thread was used for quilting but only because it was the only thread available.

Hoops

A 14" round quilting hoop is the perfect size to make cushions as well as the larger -size quilts.

Thimbles

A MUST. We teach all our quilters to use a thimble. We start them off using a leather thimble because it's less awkward and they can still feel the needle. We then tell them to try a metal thimble because it lasts longer. Also, use an under thimble for the bottom finger under the hoop.

Scissors

Paper scissors to cut out your paper designs and patterns.
Fabric scissors to cut out your quilt. Every quilter knows a sharp scissors is a must.
Clippers to cut thread. You'll be using these scissors most of the time.

Elastic and Safety Pins

One yard of 1-inch elastic cut into three equal pieces.
Three safety pins.
The elastic and safety pins will help quilt the outside edges and corners of the quilt.

Tracing Pencils

NO tracing pencils have ever been allowed in our quilting classes. We teach the quilters to find the quilting lines with their eyes and to use their fingers as their guide.

The supply list does not include fabric for binding and completing the cushion top. Quilting is very specific but there are many ways to complete the binding and make a cushion, and we leave that creativeness to the quilter.

Sewing Your Masterpiece

Preparing & joining your fabric

1. Cut your fabric to size: top design piece, backing, quilt backing, and batting. Join your fabric if necessary.

2. 22" & 45" designs—no joining necessary.

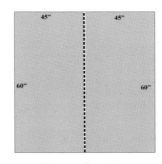

3. 60" x 90"—Join your material on its 60" length to fashion the 60" x 90" fabric.

4. 90" x 90"—You can join your fabric at the center using a 1/4" seam. Iron your seams open.

5. 90" x 90"—You can also join your fabric by using a 45" center and two 22" side panels. Iron your seams open.

6. 108" x 108"—Seam two 45" panels with a center 22" panel. Again, don't forget to iron your seams open. Some quilters like to baste them open and remove the stitches later.

Folding your fabric

1. Place your fabric on a flat surface.

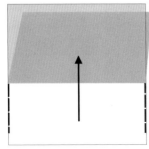

2. **Half Fold:** Fold your fabric in half, correct side of fabric in. Iron the creases of your fold.

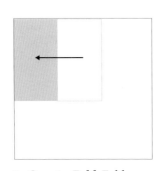

3. **Quarter Fold:** Fold your fabric in half again and iron your folds flat.

Stop at this fold for twin-size quilt 60" x 90" and wallhanging 45" x 60".

4. **1/8 Fold:** Fold your fabric into a right angle bringing all the folded edges together and iron the folds flat. You should now have a three-folded edge. Repeat for backing fabric.

Laying out your pattern & cutting your design

1. After the fabric is folded, ,some quilters prefer to either pin or base down the folds of the material so no shifting occurs during the cutting process.

2. Cut your pattern on its fold lines and place it on your top design fabric then pin. Pin from the center of the pattern out. Be sure your bias and straight are on the folds of the fabric.

3. Some quilters like to pin and even baste along the pattern line. It makes cutting out the design easier. Now cut out your pattern.

Note...
Remember sharp scissors is a must, and don't forget to cut your pattern along all the solid lines.

4. After you've completed cutting your pattern, remove your pins.

5. Place your backing fabric on a flat surface and open your design to its 1/8 fold. The creases you ironed into the back fabric should help you to center your quilt.

6. Open the design to the quarter fold. When laying out the larger quilt remember to lay seam of design on seam of backing.

7. Open the design to the half fold.

8. Open the complete design. Be sure the design is centered and pin securely in place. Start from the center and work out.

9. When laying out a design with a border, lay out the border first.

10. Then lay out the center design. Now pin your design to the backing fabric. Start from the center and work to the outer edge of the design.

11. Begin basting your design to the backing fabric, 1/4" in from the outside edge. Remove the pins.

12. You may need to baste within the design of very large motifs to hold the fabric down securely.

Appliquéing

1. Using "Sharp" needles for appliqué, thread your needle and knot the end of your thread. Measure the length of your thread from shoulder to finger tips.

2. You are now ready to appliqué. Never begin at a valley or a point. Start on a long edge. With the tip of your needle, tuck a small section of material under to the basting line.

3. Now drag the side of the needle neatly folding the fabric under.

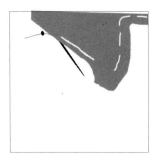

4. Push your needle between the folds of the top fabric and come out through the edge of the fold hiding your knot.

Note...
The stitches on the following graphics were purposely made larger to show the appliqué stitch. A good appliquer's stitch will be difficult to see—almost invisible.

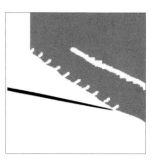

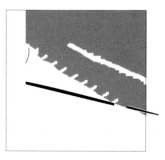

5. Appliqué stitch: Place your threaded needle under the last stitch on the background fabric.

6. Pick up the background fabric, come back up through the folded edge of the top material, and push your needle through. Your stitches should be 1/8" apart from each other. Repeat.

7. Points: Sew 1/8" from the point or one stitch before the point. Your last stitch will become your new point.

8. Now mitre your fabric by tucking the point under your last stitch.

9. Begin to tuck your fabric from the tip of your last stitch down the other edge. Tug your thread a little and your point should reappear.

10. Inner Corner: Tuck and sew all the way into the valley but DO NOT tuck the other edge of the valley.

11. Only after you've reached the inside point of the valley do you begin to tuck the other edge. The fabric should automatically fold under.

12. After your quilt is completely appliquéd, remove the basting stitch. Check your backing; there should be no long strings hanging out the back.

13. Joining your batting: If you need to join your batting, cut to size and then place the batting side by side on a table, NOT one on top the other. Whip stitch the two sections together.

Quilting

1. Lay out the backing fabric on a flat surface, then the batting, and finally the completed appliqué piece on top. Center and pin.

2. Baste all three layers together starting from the middle and then 5 inches apart, working toward the outside edge.

3. Repeat in the other direction. Your quilt should eventual look like a grid. This keeps the batting from shifting during quilting.

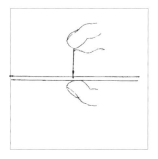

4. When basting a smaller cushion top, just baste around the edge. All other sizes need to be grid basted.

5. Quilt the center first. Place your quilt on a hoop. The bottom ring of the hoop should be behind the fabric and the top ring on top of the fabric. Smooth out the fabric on the front and on the back of the hoop. You need to do this to avoid puckering.

6. Your first quilting stitch is hidden within the batting. Push your needle through your fabric about a 1" away from your starting point. Push your thread through the batting, and not the backing, to your starting point. Push the knot through. Now you're ready to begin quilting.

7. Quilting stitch: Place your needle in front of the previous stitch. Poke through all three layers, gently touching your bottom finger. You will be quilting toward yourself.

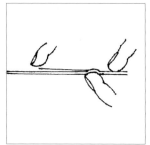

8. Rock your needle all the way back away from you, touching the top material with the back of the needle. Push up the front of needle by pushing up the back finger under the hoop.

9. Place your thumb just in front of your bottom finger and right in front of where the needle will come through. This is to help cut off the stitch. Push the needle through. Now make another stitch. "Repeat."

10. To end your quilt stitch simply, make a knot close to the end of the last stitch next to the fabric. Make one final stitch but bring your needle through the batting, and not the backing, 1" away from the last stitch. Push the knot through the top fabric.

11. **Quilts with an open center:** Quilt the ditch first. The ditch is the line on the edge of the backing fabric next to where the design begins. Then quilt in another row.

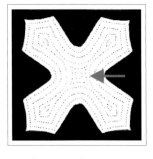

12. Then quilt in rows toward the center of the quilt.

13. **Finger spacing:** Use your fingers as your space measure—no larger than the width of your index finger or smaller then your baby finger.

14. **Closed centers:** Start at the edges of the center of the quilt.

15. Then quilt in rows toward the center of the quilt.

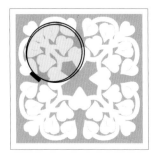

16. Quilt the design next.

17. Consistency in stitches is what's important but we tell our quilters to strive for 10-12 top stitches per inch.

18. When quilting you can use the echo quilting style, the wave-like quilt design.

19. Use the definitive quilting style to make the design look like the exact image.

20. After you have quilted your design, don't forget to quilt in the ditch outlining your design on the background fabric. Try to hide the stitch under the appliqué.

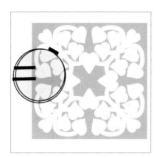

21. After your design is completely quilted, begin to quilt the outside edge.

22. Use the elastic and safety pins to help quilt the edges of the quilt. Wrap the elastic around the hoop, pull the elastic to the fabric, and pin to the edge of the quilt with the pin on top and the elastic behind.

23. The final quilting stitch is the edge of the quilt. This can be done without a hoop. Cut off any excess batting and fabric.

24. Bind your quilt. There are so many different ways to bind a quilt—we leave that creativeness to you.

> *Note...*
> Don't forget to label and document your quilt. You can attach a label to the back of the quilt or even add decorative lettering on the binding. Tell the quilt's story by naming the quilt, the date it was completed, whom it was made for, and who quilted it.

Reverse Appliqué

1. Place your fabric on a flat surface.

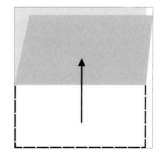

2. Half Fold: Fold your fabric in half, correct side of fabric in. Those making the larger quilts, your seams should be facing out. Iron the creases of your fold.

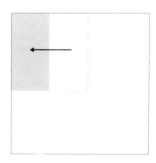

3. Quarter Fold: Fold your fabric in half again and iron your folds flat.

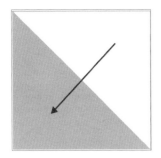

4. 1/8 Fold: Fold your fabric into a right angle bringing all the folded edges together and iron the folds flat. You should now have a three-folded edge.

5. Cut out your pattern on its angles, place on top your design fabric, and pin. Using a rotary cutter, press down on the fabric to make the initial cut. Then, using small clippers, carefully cut on the solid line.

6. When you've finish cutting the pattern, remove the pins. Lay out your background fabric on a flat surface and then completely open the top design fabric on the backing and pin.

7 Baste around each individual slit and the outer edge of the fabric.

8. Appliqué the slits open. A small tuck will give a more subtle design, and a deeper tuck will make the design bolder.

9. When the appliqué is complete. Join the top piece, batting, and backing, and begin quilting. Again start in the middle and work your way out to the edge like you would quilt a regular quilt.

Note...

Again start in the middle and work your way out to the edge like you would quilt a regular quilt.

Words to Sew by...

• Use sharp scissors.

• Sew every day. Make time to sew at least one hour every day and you can complete a cushion in 2-3 weeks, a wallhanging in 3-6 months, and a large quilt in one year.

• Choose colors you enjoy.

• Join a quilting class or quilt guild near you for encouragement and friendship.

Pattern for a 22" x 22" Cushion or Wallhanging

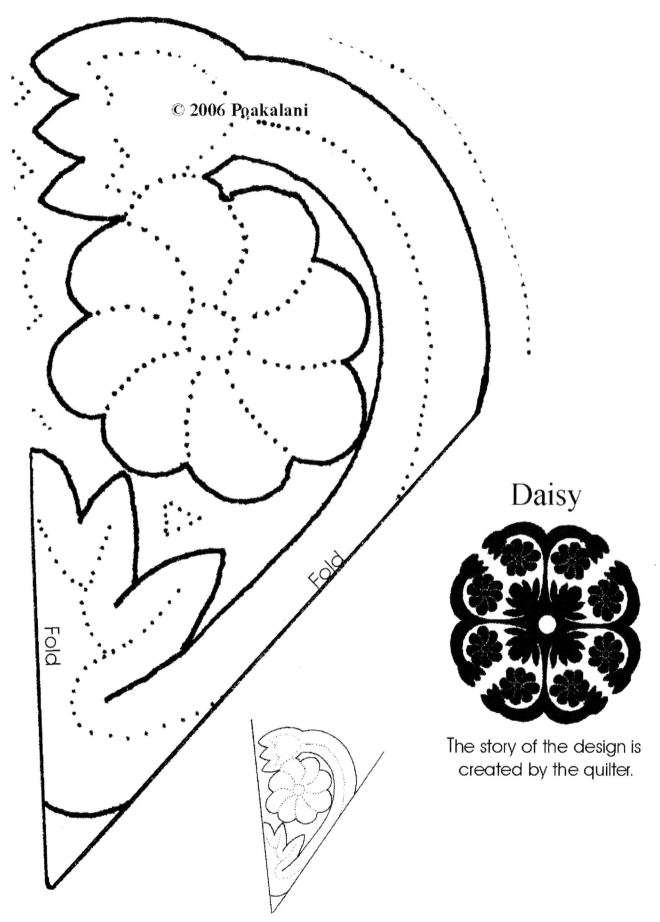

© 2006 Poakalani

Fold

Fold

Daisy

The story of the design is created by the quilter.

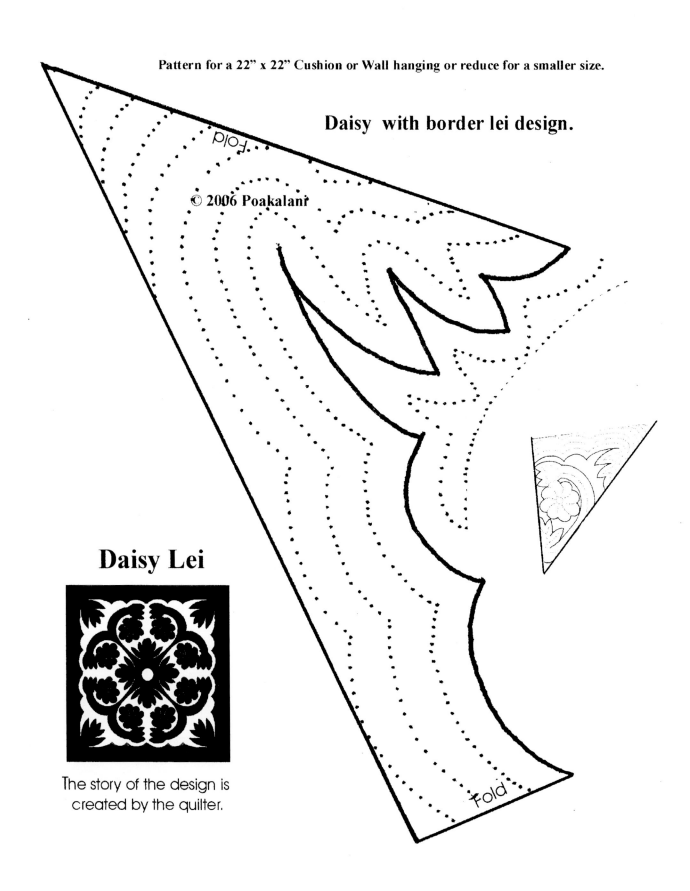

Pattern for a 22" x 22" Cushion or Wall hanging or reduce for a smaller size.

Daisy with border lei design.

© 2006 Poakalani

Fold

Fold

Fold

Daisy Lei

The story of the design is
created by the quilter.

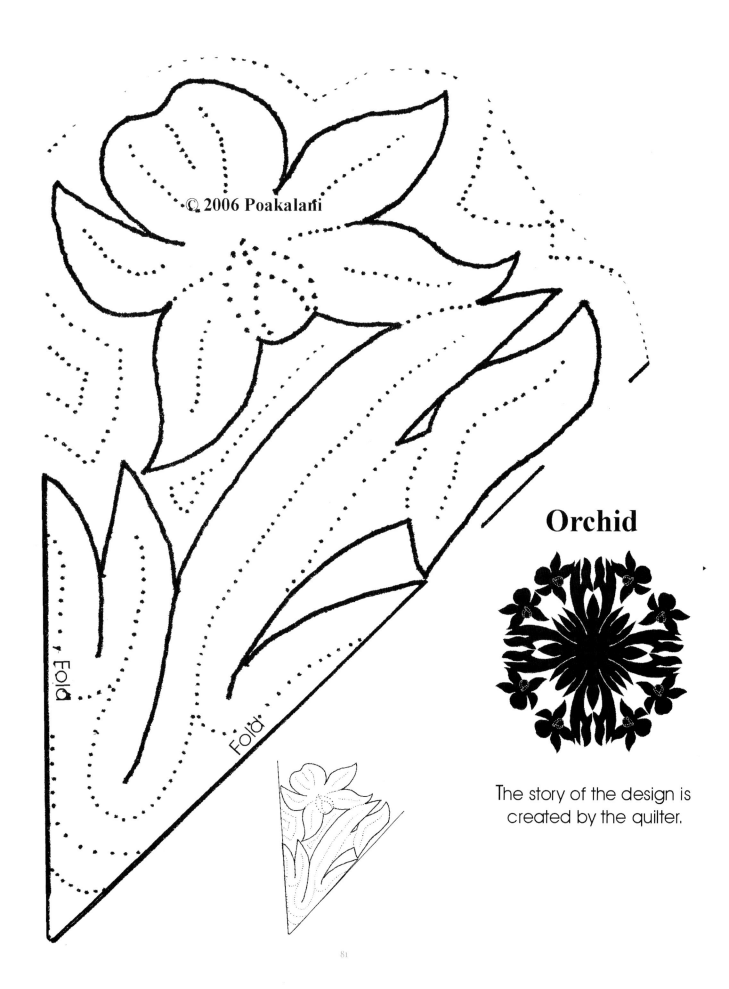

© 2006 Poakalani

Fold

Fold

Orchid

The story of the design is created by the quilter.

Pattern for a 22" x 22" Cushion or Wallhanging
Orchid with border lei design.

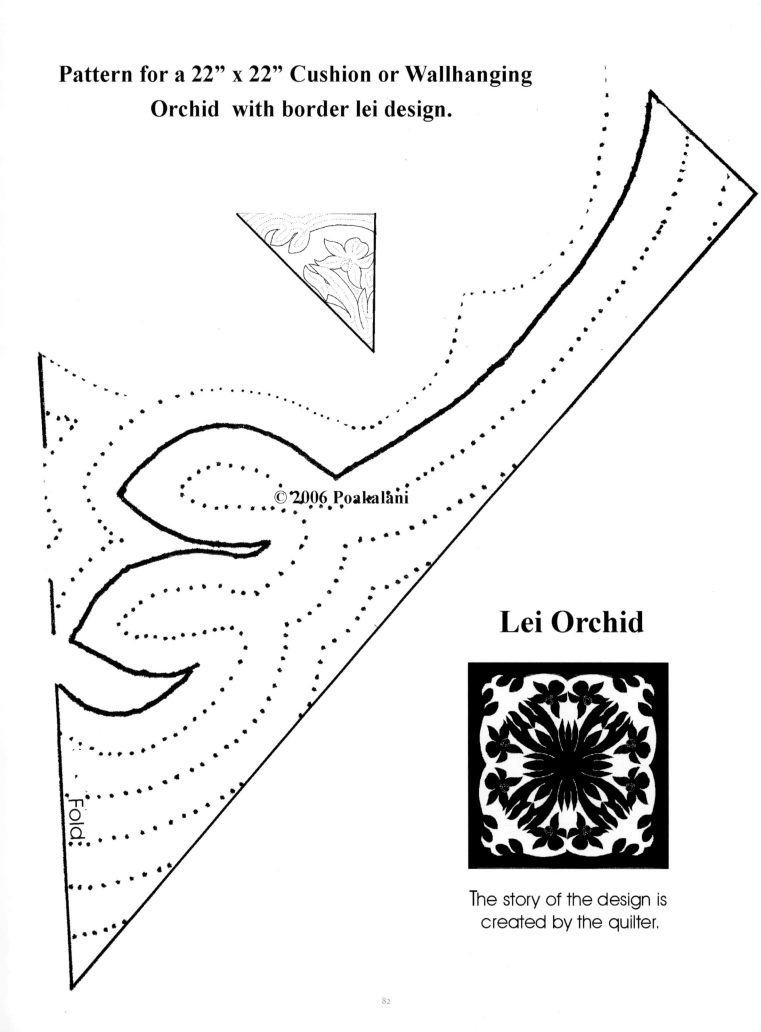

© 2006 Poakalani

Fold

Lei Orchid

The story of the design is
created by the quilter.

Pattern for a 22" x 22" Cushion or Wallhanging

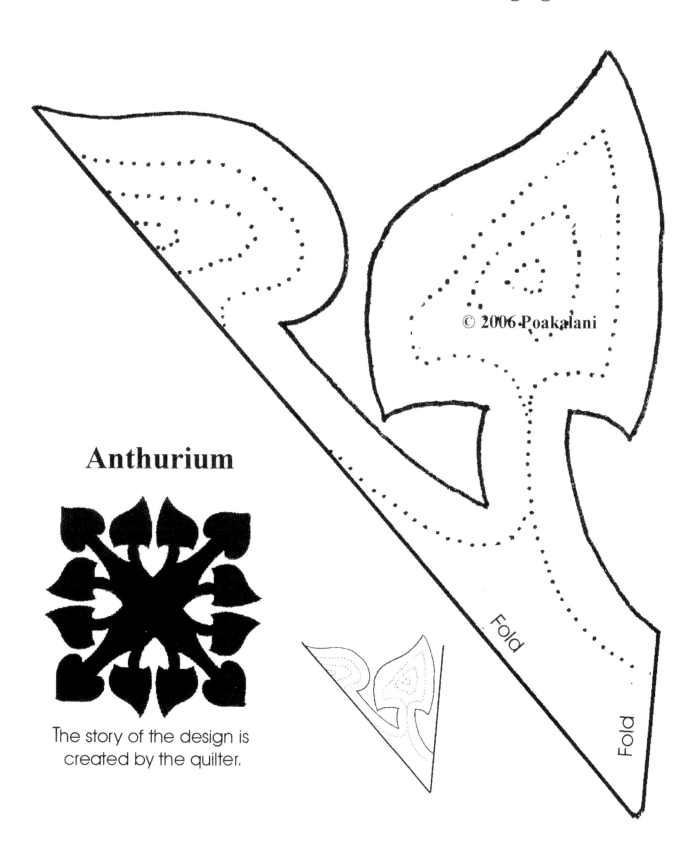

© 2006 Poakalani

Anthurium

The story of the design is created by the quilter.

Fold

Fold

Pattern for a 22" x 22" Cushion or Wallhanging
Anthurium with border lei design.

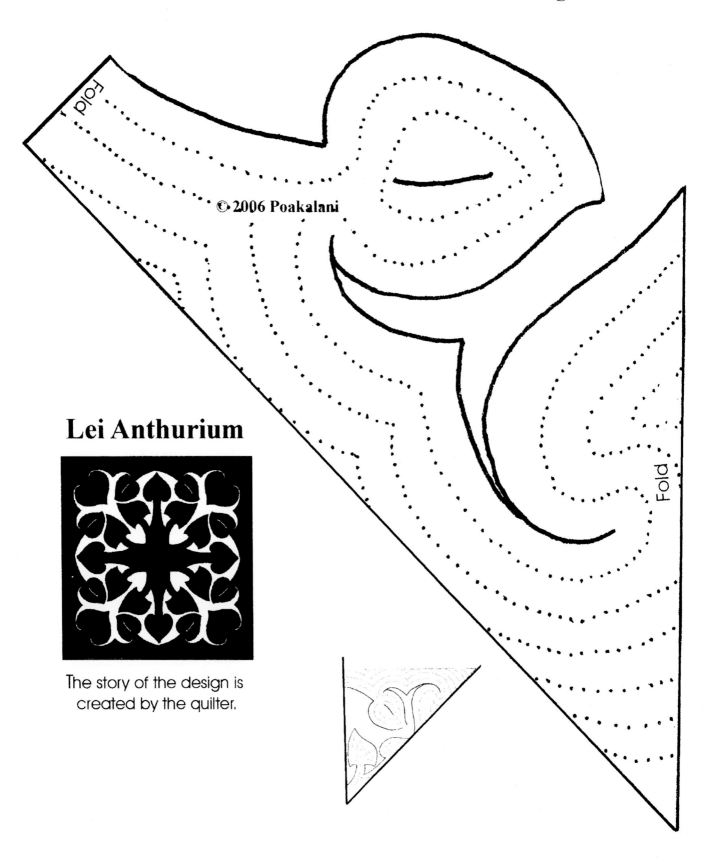

© 2006 Poakalani

Fold

Fold

Fold

Lei Anthurium

The story of the design is
created by the quilter.

Pattern for a 22" x 22" Cushion or Wallhanging

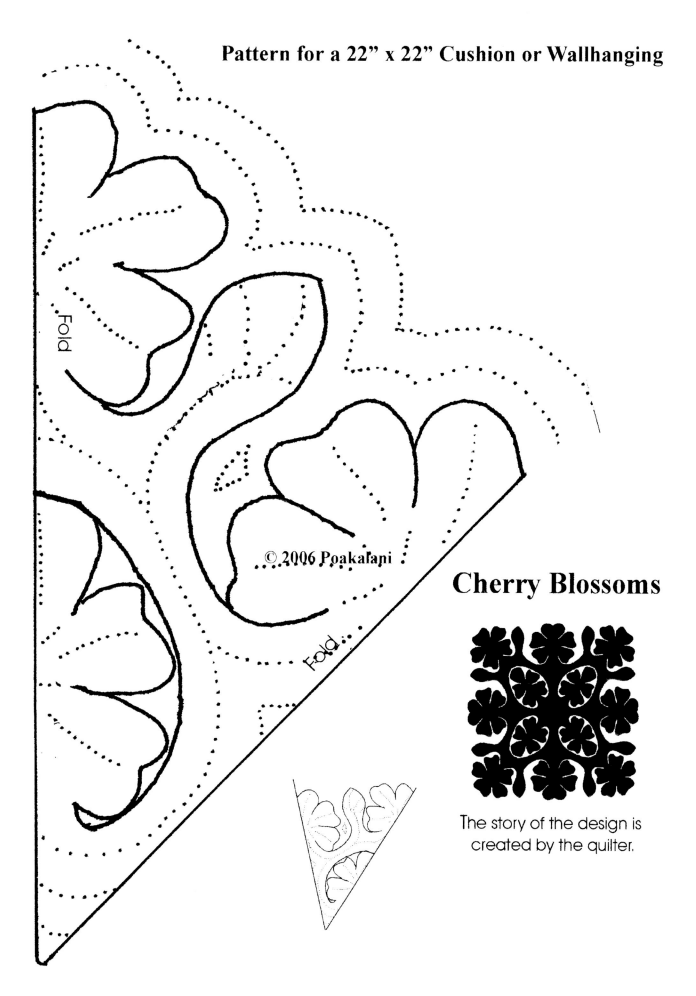

Fold

© 2006 Poakalani

Fold

Cherry Blossoms

The story of the design is created by the quilter.

Pattern for a 45" x 45" Wallhanging

© 2006 Poakalani

Fold

Fold

Anthurium

The story of the design is created by the quilter.

Increase Pattern approx. 240% for a 45" x 45" wall hanging or leave original size for miniature quilts.

Kalo

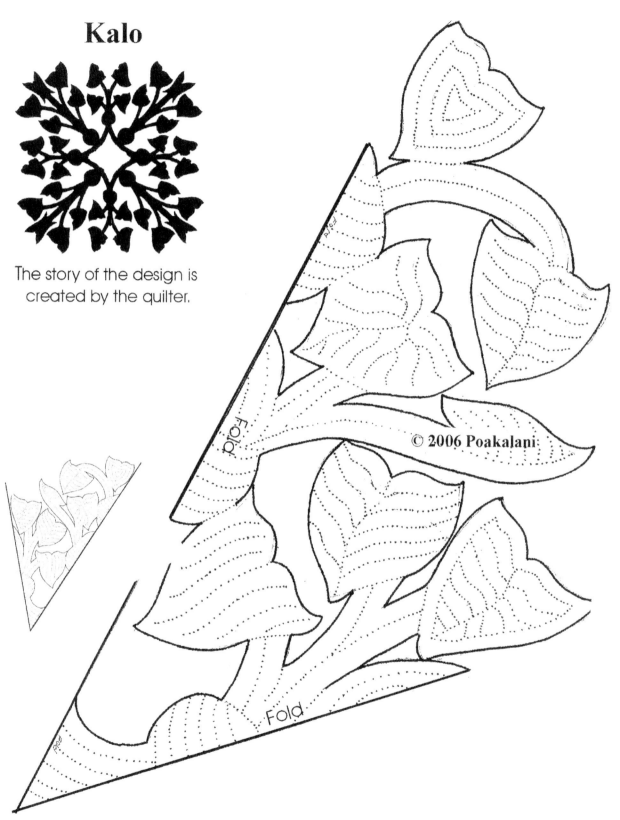

The story of the design is created by the quilter.

© 2006 Poakalani

Fold

Fold

Fold

Increase pattern approx. 240% for a 45" x 45" wall hanging or leave original size for miniature quilts.

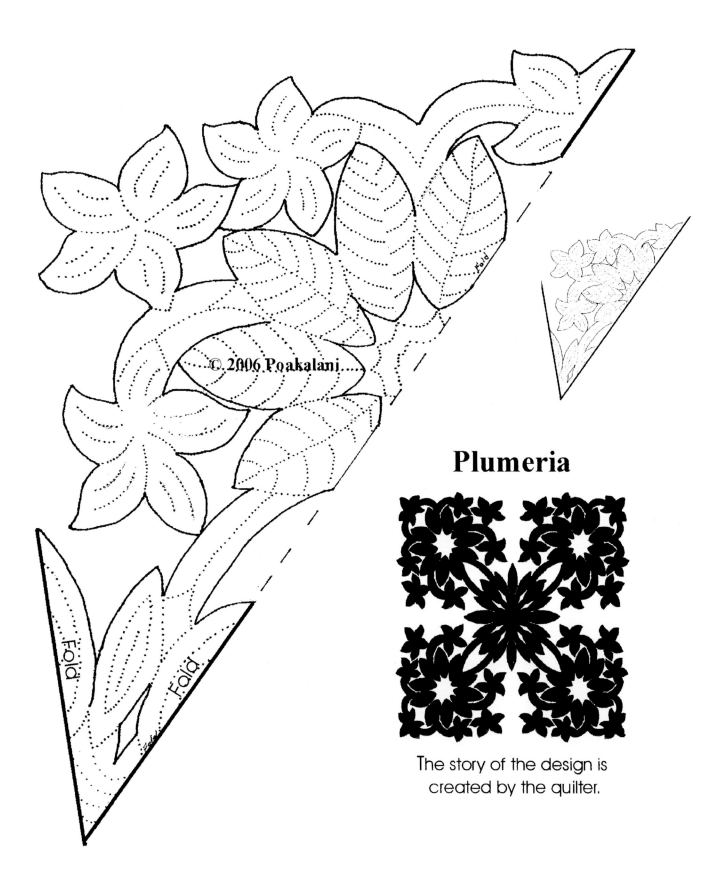

© 2006 Poakalani

Plumeria

The story of the design is created by the quilter.

Increase pattern approx. 240% for a 45" x 45" wall hanging or leave original size for miniature quilts.

Hearts & Roses

The story of the design is
created by the quilter.

© 2006 Poakalani

Fold

Fold

Increase pattern approx. 240% for a 45" x 45" wall hanging or leave original size
for miniature quilts.

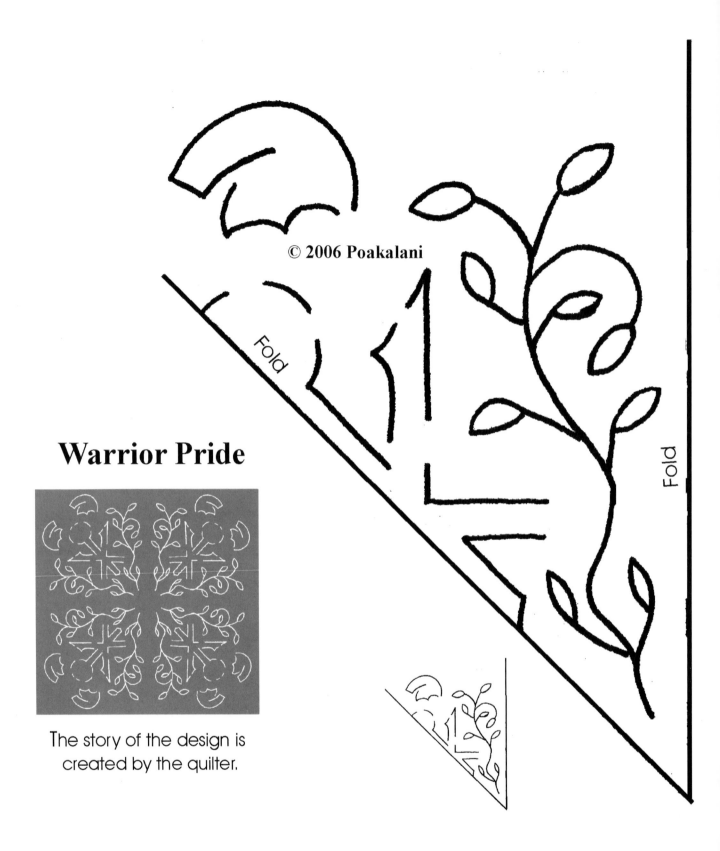

© 2006 Poakalani

Fold

Fold

Warrior Pride

The story of the design is created by the quilter.

Increase Pattern approx. 240% for a 45" x 45" wall hanging or leave original size for miniature quilts. Designs can also be used as individual stencils on traditional and contemporary Hawaiian quilts.

© 2006 Poakalani

Hawaiian Flag

The story of the design is created by the quilter.

Increase Pattern approx. 240% for a 45" x 45" wall hanging or leave original size for miniature quilts. Designs can also be used as individual stencils on traditional and contemporary Hawaiian quilts.

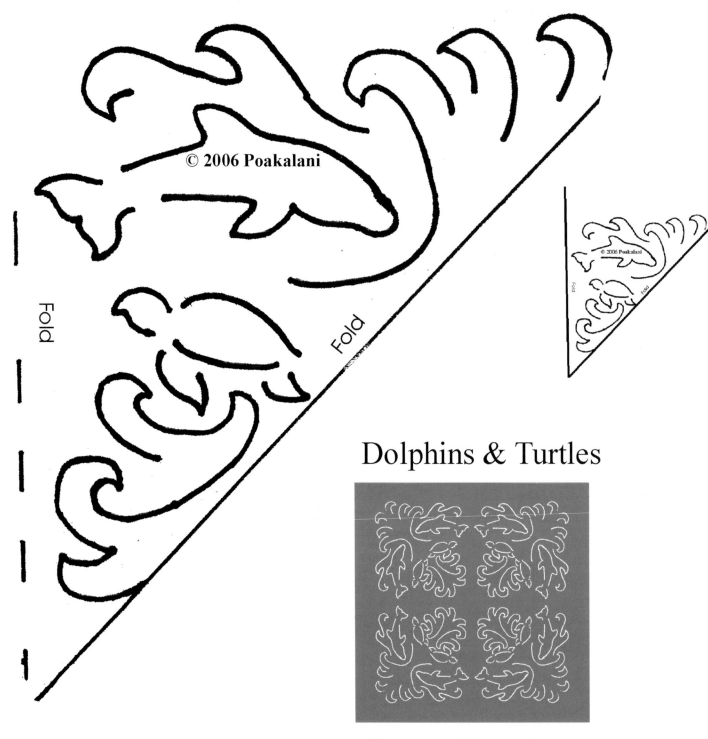

© 2006 Poakalani

Fold

Fold

Dolphins & Turtles

The story of the design is
created by the quilter.

Increase Pattern approx. 240% for a 45" x 45" wall hanging or leave original size for miniature quilts. Designs can also be used as individual stencils on traditional and contemporary Hawaiian quilts.

Tropical Island

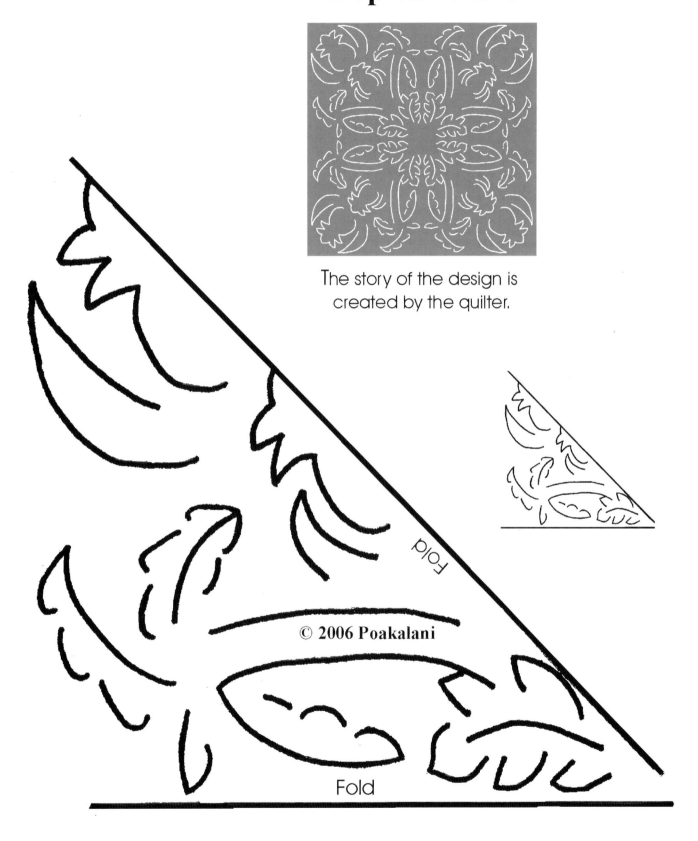

The story of the design is created by the quilter.

Fold

© 2006 Poakalani

Fold

Increase Pattern approx. 240% for a 45" x 45" wall hanging or leave original size for miniature quilts. Designs can also be used as individual stencils on traditional and contemporary Hawaiian quilts.

Photo Album

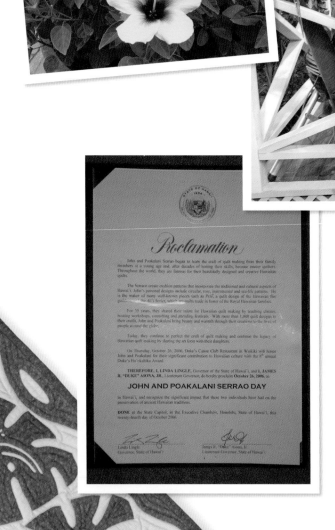

Glossary

Ali'i	*High chiefs of old Hawai'i*
'Aumakua	*Family spirit guide*
Appliquéing	*Process of sewing the top material design to a backing fabric*
'Awapuhi	*Ginger flower*
Baste	*Temporary stitches about 1/2" in length to secure the design to the backing fabric*
Batting	*Polyester, wool, or cotton filling used as a middle layer for a quilt*
Bias	*The line crossing over the straight of the fabric*
Commercial Designs	*Patterns available on the commercial market*
Cross Hatching	*Quilting lines designed like a checkerboard*
Definitive Quilting	*Quilting lines defining the pattern to represent the design to its closest likeness*
Ditch	*The outside edge of the design between the pattern and the backing material*
Echo Quilting	*Quilting lines following the design of the pattern*
Haku Lei	*A woven floral wreath*
Hinahina	*Silversword found only on the slopes of Haleakalā and Mauna Kea*
Honu	*Turtle*
Ipu	*Gourd drums used to accompany chants and hula dancers*
'Ilima	*A bright orange paper-like flower—thousands are needed to make one lei*
Kāhili	*Feather standards used like flag and banners in old Hawai'i*
Kapa Pohopoho	*Crazy quilt*

Kukui Nut	*Also known as the candlenut tree—the oil was used for the old Hawaiian lanterns, the nut for medicinal purposes*
Laua'e	*Island fern*
Lehua	*A red or yellow flower that looks similar to a barbers' shaving brush honoring Pele*
Lei Niho Palaoa	*Necklace worn by high ranking chiefs, made from whales' teeth shaped like a hook and attached to strands of human hair; believed to ward off evil thoughts*
Loke Lani	*Heavenly rose, Queen Emma's favorite flower*
Mahele	*Law decreed by Kamehameha III dividing the lands of Hawai'i for private ownership*
Mahiole	*Hawaiian helmet*
Mokihana	*A green berry with the scent of anise, strung like beads and woven to make lei*
Pahu	*Hawaiian drum used to accompany hula dancers and chants*
Personal Quilt Design	*Personal quilt patterns made exclusively for one quilter*
Pua Pākē (Chinese Flower)	*Chrysanthemum; favorite flower of the Chinese plantation workers*
Sampler Quilt	*A quilt using several block designs*
Reverse Appliqué	*A style of quilting where slits are made to create a design*
Tapa	*Hawai'i's fabric, originally from tree bark, used for clothing and bed coverings*
Tuck	*To fold the edges of the material under*
Tūtū	*Grandmother*
'Ukulele	*Literally means jumping flea, a four-string Hawaiian instrument*
'Ūlei Berries	*Grow on a woody shrub used to make digging sticks*
'Ulī'ulī	*Feather gourd used as a hula implement, very similar to an upside-down maracas decorated with feathers*
'Ulu	*Fruit eaten as a starch in Hawai'i and the Pacific Islands*

About the Authors

ALTHEA POAKALANI SERRAO was born with only one hand. Raised by her grandmother Caroline Correa, a master quilter and designer, Poakalani was only able to watch the quilters because it was thought that she would hurt herself with the needles. It was only after her grandmother had passed away and she had a family of her own that Poakalani was finally able to look into the quilt patterns she inherited from her grandmother. Poakalani and her husband, John, viewed the quilt patterns. Both felt that it was easier to learn on a smaller quilt, so they created the first 30 cushion patterns in their collection conforming to the traditional and cultural aspects of old Hawai'i. It was at this time that Poakalani appeared to have found her gift as a quilter. Using the knowledge of her childhood, she found that even with only one hand she had the skill of an accomplished quilter. In 1972 Poakalani began to demonstrate Hawaiian quilting statewide and eventually taught her own weekly quilting classes. Poakalani expressed her feelings about teaching the art of the Hawaiian quilting, stating that the art should be taught to all who were interested whether they were Hawaiian or just Hawaiian at heart.

JOHN SERRAO was raised watching his mother and grandmother quilt and design Hawaiian quilts. It was not of great interest to him then but it would become part of his life after his retirement from the Honolulu Police Department. After his retirement, John often helped his wife with her quilting classes. While the quilters often used the commercial patterns he originally designed, they wanted their own personal Hawaiian quilt design. One day they asked John to make a larger bed-size quilt design. So he picked up a pencil and designed his first large quilt. You could say the rest is history. John has become and is known today as Hawai'i's top quilt designer. He has designed well over 1,000 quilt designs that can be found locally as well as worldwide on quilts, logos, fabric, stationary, stencils, and even T-shirts. John also conducts quilt design workshops so the art of designing can be passed on to anyone who is willing to learn. He has become a Hawaiian quilt consultant, historian, and cultural artist. John's designs are not only based on the flora, culture, and history of Hawai'i but also the spiritual essence of the quilters themselves.

RAELENE CORREIA (a.k.a. Tuffy) is an integral part of the classes. Her business contacts and organizational skills have kept the classes running smoothly for the past 16 years. She is the go-to person in a crisis. While Poakalani, John, and Cissy concentrate on teaching, Raelene, who also teaches, focuses on keeping the classes within the traditional and cultural integrity on which they were founded.

CISSY SERRAO has been teaching Hawaiian quilting along side her parents for the past 16 years. While Cissy enjoys teaching, she has also played an important role in the preservation of Hawaiian quilting by publishing the first Hawaiian quilting website on the Internet. Her website is now *the* resource for Hawaiian quilting. She is also known for her quilting instructions, and several of her articles have been published in various quilting magazines and books. Cissy is fast becoming a quilt historian and consultant.

POAKALANI HAWAIIAN QUILTING CLASSES

The quilters and students of Poakalani's classes meet weekly at various venues in Honolulu. The classes are a blend of learning the art of quilting and a circle of friendship. No tracing pencils are allowed in the classes. Beginner students start with a cushion kit and learn to baste, appliqué, and quilt their first cushion top. After completing their first quilted top (and only if their stitches are consistent and neat), they are allowed to continue to the larger quilts. It is at this time that John sits down with the student to help them design their own personal quilt and story. John only designs quilts for his quilting class because he knows that they not only understand the technique of sewing but also the history and tradition of the quilts. You can reach Poakalani & Company at www.poakalani.com, email: quilt@poakalani.com, or call: (808) 521-1568.